REAL ESTATE INVESTOR

Learn how to invest in real estate to create your passive income with rental property investing, commercial real estate and more.

By George Tower

Disclaimer

All erudition supplied in this book are specified for educational and academic purpose only. The author is not in any way in charge for any outcomes that emerge from using this book. Constructive efforts have been made to render information that is both precise and effective, however the author is not to be held answerable for the accuracy or use/misuse of this information.

Foreword

I will like to thank you for taking the very first step of trusting me and deciding to purchase/read this life-transforming book. Thanks for investing your time and resources on this product.

I can assure you of precise outcomes if you will diligently follow the specific blueprint I lay bare in the information handbook you are currently checking out. It has transformed lives, and I strongly believe it will equally transform your own life too. All the information I provided in this Do It Yourself piece is easy to absorb and practice.

Table of Contents

INTRODUCTION

It isn't just a case of speculating to accumulate. You need to learn when to buy and when to walk away, and that's the hard point that some people who invest in real estate don't watch for. This can be the distinction between generating income and losing your investment. In this book, I will describe exactly how you can make your experience as a house customer or as a possible house fin effective. You will discover everything about buying homes at deal costs, concerning the research that you need to take into the market, and how this research study settles long-term.

Having little cash to buy real estate, but being a serious-minded individual, I could get properties at fairly low cost and get to know the market, to ensure that I can market these on and make a good-looking revenue. What I found out on the trip was fascinating. It isn't just a situation of hypothesizing to gather. You do have to know what you are trying to find and you also need to recognize what it will certainly cost you to make the property that you have purchased fit a details market.

It isn't as simple as buying a house and building it up. The real estate market is more complicated than that. You need to keep in mind the state of the market, the location of the market that you are, the price of repair and the total size of time that you will have your cash locked up in the property. With the best perspective of the real estate market, it can be an advantageous means of generating income. Without proficiency and without taking safety measures, it can be a catastrophe. This book will help you to know how it works and what you can do to make sure that your real estate gives you the best return. You will indeed discover everything about what you are looking for in a new property to make sure that you stay clear of some of the usual challenges.

You need to know as much as you can around its income and expenditures if you're thinking about buying an income property. As we will highlight throughout this book, you are not genuinely buying a physical property, but you are buying its income stream. The elegance is in the lower line.

If you're taking into consideration the buying of an income property, the information you get will possibly be either straight from the seller or indirectly, via the seller's representative. In the chapters, you'll see substantial information on how to evaluate the standard income and expenditure amounts, but, your first worry below is, "Are they the same?" Right here are some way that can help you figure out whether you're an expert income-property investor or a beginner just examining the waters for the first time, this book will certainly tell you how to "run the numbers" on any type of real estate investment. It is created to work as an indispensable overview and referral.

Like all kinds of investing, real estate requires that you establish expertise with some standard dimensions prices of return, capital, and estimates of worth, among others. The objective of this book is to clarify how to make these estimations for virtually any kind of income property and to explain the standard idea behind each estimate of how to make you a smarter investor. Without recognizing these essential solutions, you're merely thinking when you attempt to find out whether a provided property is a significant investment. You might believe you have a successful property because it produces outstanding rental income, yet when you analyze it more thoroughly using a few of the rules in this book, you will realize that what you have is a loser.

CHAPTER ONE

What is Real Estate Investing

The question, "What is real estate investing?" cannot be addressed without thinking about first, it's academic meaning, and afterwards, it's theoretical interpretation.

The Academic Definition

Real estate has been defined as land (or stationary property) in addition to anything fixed firmly to the land such as structures, and investment is the act of using cash to buy property for the single objective of renting or holding for income. It is risk-free to say after that (incorporating both meanings) that real estate investing comprises the purchase of real estate (or investment in real estate) for objectives of producing earnings, making a profit, and getting richer.

The Conceptual Definition

Leverages, in contrast to stock investment investments (which normally call for more equity from the investor), it is possible to use a real estate investment. With a real estate investment, you can use other people's cash to amplify your rate of return and manage a more prominent investment or else not possible.

Tax Shelter Real estate investing gives tax obligation advantages. There are returns on yearly after-tax capital, equity build-up with recognition of the possession, and after-tax capital obligation on sale.

Non-Monetary Returns Real estate investment gives the satisfaction of possession, the protection that you manage the property, and profile diversity

Real estate investing is not a bed of roses. Real estate investment calls for funding, there are dangers, and rental property can be management-intensive. On the other hand, the cars you drive necessary funding, it includes risk driving, and it calls for management. The difference is that the vehicle is not a source of wealth.

How to Become a Real Estate Investor

Make a real estate investment goal. What do you wish to achieve, and by when do you intend to achieve it? What rate of return do you want to get on the cash you take out of your houses or checking account to get an investment property provided the risk?

-Discover what returns you must seek, and just how to calculate them. You can not do well in music unless you can read songs. Buy an excellent real estate investment software application where you can discover how to run the returns and calculate the formulas.

-Watch out for getting Rich systems. There are many so-called gurus ready to teach you how to make millions with real estate investment property. But let logic be your guide; we believe that nobody who finds a gold mine publishes a map.

-Produce a connection with a real estate expert that knows the regional real estate market and knows rental property. It will not improve your investment goals to hang out with the "professional real estate of the year" unless that person learns about investment property and is adequately prepared to assist you in acquiring it. Get a professional that comprehends real estate investing.

Real estate investing is a business about owning a piece of ground that, when researched and purchased sensibly by equal numbers and careful management, and with reasonable objectives and caution, will likely be more valuable tomorrow than it is today.

Real Estate Basics

You get in the real estate market the minute that you get your first houses. To acquire that house, you need to have established your financial resources approximately have the ability to pay your current expenses and to any kind of costs that are sustained at the new area. As you possess the property, whether you are purchasing it to turn or to occupy, you are in charge of the drives and all tax-related to that property.

Make sure you check the market before purchasing. You wish to have a contrast before making a deal. That means that you can value one investment against one more. Some people with little cash to spend might choose to pick a property that requires fixings over a longer time. The fact that your house is in a poor state of repair work will mean that the rate on the market will have been reasonably reduced the technique yet is exercising what the property would deserve when every one of these repair services is done and what the price of those repair services is most likely to be.

In real estate, you have different kinds of sales. When you can get, short sales are property at less than the quantity that the seller is indebted to the financial institution. In an instance like this, the financial institution might have surrendered on ever returning the amount owed and might concur that the seller can make the sale to settle as long as your house is most likely to realize.

The issue with a short sale is that they do not always turn out to be a fantastic house as the buyers think it will be. There might be repair work needed that is excessive, yet buyers enter thoughtlessly because they look like they are getting a great deal.

A home inspection costs money, but it doesn't cost as much as the potential loss that you can make if you buy a short sale property that needs more care than its worth.

-Auction properties-- These are typically residential or commercial properties that have been seized. The current owner can not afford to pay the financial institution, and the financial institution wants their cash back.

Now, these can mean a real bargain if you know what damages need fixing and you are aware of the market, can be a real deal. We will go into this later, but mostly these are houses the financial institution is ready to cost the quantity owed on a particular day. The benefit of these sales is that you can get deals. The negative aspect is that you need to have checked the property in a short space of time and must have the finance in place before you bid. The mistake that people make with this kind of acquisition is that they offered over their budget plan and leave much less cash for fixings.

Sales via real estate agent-- These are houses that have been sold for some reason. Maybe the owners are relocating to a new community. Possibly they are merely relocating to bigger house. When it comes to senior citizens, these elders might be moving right into relieved living and do not need a large house anymore. There can be all sorts of reasons a house comes into the market. The benefit of this type of sale is that you can typically know the history of your property and have even more time to make a decision and examine the worth of the houses.

Because the real estate agent will act as an intermediary between you and the seller, you also have more negotiating power.

For a rental investment, the downside is that it locks up your first cash, and unless you have more money for your next investment, this might not be a good move. If you have excess money to spend, you might discover that you will be able to recover any kind of home mortgage repayments from occupants, which means that the investment pays for itself over some time.

Deciding on Your Budget.

You need to know how much you can invest when you go into the real estate market. This must consist of the price of the houses in addition to the legal costs, agency costs, adequate cash to refurbish your home as required, and put it back into the market. While

you possess your house, it will get no earnings and will be a responsibility. Your budget plan needs to consist of a fixed time where you will be expected to pay the mortgage if any work is required to be completed. People typically forget this facet of expense, but monthly that you have your house will certainly cost you cash and need to be counted.

Bear in mind what the financial institution is ready to give you and what this will cost you during the time that you own the property. You can pay for a house insurance policy through that you have the property and understand what tax put on your ownership.

You need to have a precise cap on what you can manage to invest because this allows you just to check out houses that fall under your range price and a little higher, keeping in mind that there is always space for arrangement. It helps to be able to get a contractor to give you first quotes on the price to do any kind of repair services on the property. Remodeling can be needed yet pricey to appreciate the houses or to fix appliances in the property that need to be in excellent functioning order. Relying on the job that needs to be done, you might require to seek advice from plumbings, electrical experts, or merely necessary contractors to get the most effective quotes and concepts for repairs.

Inspecting

- House

When you inspect houses, be aware that in the area where apartments are located, there may be a lot of houses for sale. If this is the case, look at the competition. See what homes are selling and for what price. Getting friendly with a real estate agent will help you because if they think that you will give them your business, they will be happy to provide you with information.

There are several things that you need to take into account when you inspect a home. These are as follows:

- The expense of re-wiring a first three-bedroom house
- The price of rewiring a two bedroomed home
- The expense of mounting a kitchen area right into X

Various other manner ins that you can reduce your budget plan is to establish accounts at your regional shops to ensure that you are qualified for discount rates for materials, lumber, components, and various other repair needs. This will certainly assist you to save cash. Contractor's shops that market drywall surface and all of the products required for the repair must be able to supply you a charge account. This permits you to allocate the costs instead of having sticker label shock at the expense of products per journey.

Getting Ready to Make an Offer

Several things will tell you how desperate someone is to sell a home. Signs that there is room for negotiation in the price are the following:

- The house has been on the market a long time
- The house is rated too high compared with other properties in the area
- There are repairs to be done that will be expensive
- The owners have already moved out so are desperate to break relations with their past life
- The home has been neglected

These are all specific items, but they give you a clue about the property, and they also tell you whether the home is likely to sell at its actual price. The real estate agent will be able to tell you if the price has been dropped recently. They will also be able to talk to you about the situations of the seller. Be friendly. Learn as much as you can because all this information can help you to get a bargain.

When you have your property report, you will be able to make a more detailed assessment of what it will cost to do any renovations that may be needed, although that may not stop you from making an offer. If there is a lot of interest in the home, you may be able to make a hesitant offer, bearing in mind the repairs that you have already noted with a provision that the offer is subject to a satisfactory property report. That covers you in case there is something drastic that you didn't pick up on when you were looking around the house.

If you are dealing with buying the house through a real estate agent, you should never make the offer directly with the seller. Talk things reasonably with the real estate agent.

The real estate agent will have been working with the seller and should have a good idea of whether your offer comes anywhere near the amount that the seller needs. You get more information from real estate agents because selling the house is their main priority.

However, don't be communicated into something that your instinct tells you is a higher price than you are ready to pay because you will inevitably stand to lose more. The usual procedure is for the real estate agent to contact the seller and to come back to you either with a counteroffer, which you can walk away from or details of what the seller is likely to accept.

When you are making offers on houses, you may find that you are left with this sense of expectation. Do not call again. It shows the real estate agent that you are too keen, and that's not a good thing. If you show all your cards, you leave yourself vulnerable, and it's not worth it. There will always be another house and another possibility. Do not be talked into paying more for the home than you feel it is worth, bearing in mind the checks you have done against other houses and also the number of repairs you would have to do to get the house up to the same condition as houses that are selling for more money. The more you give away at this stage, the less chance you have of turning a profit.

When you are looking for a house to live in rather than to flip, you should still look from a commercial viewpoint. This is probably the most significant investment you will make in your life. At a later stage in life, you may want to sell it. If it takes you an absolute fortune to get it into shape, you may not get your money back, and it's not worth getting yourself into that situation in the first place. If you have doubts about the costs and are being pushed to make a higher offer, walk away.

Be sure of what you are getting into, and don't sign anything until you have all the facts and are happy with them.

CHAPTER TWO

How to Analyze Deals

You need to know as much as you can about its earnings and costs if you're considering the purchase of a rental property. As we will highlight throughout this book, you are not purchasing a physical residential or commercial property, but you are buying its income stream. The beauty is in the bottom line.

If you're thinking about the purchase of an earnings residential or commercial property, the information you get will probably come either directly from the seller or indirectly, through the seller's agent.

Here are some ways that can help you discover if a property is real.

Ask to See the Leases.

There are many great reasons to do this. For one, if you purchase the property, you are going to be subjected to the term to those leases, so it's an excellent idea to know what they say. Even more to the instant factor, nevertheless, is the question of the rental prices. Do the leases agree with the seller's representations? How many times does each lease run? Do lessees have alternatives to restore, and at what prices? The solution to these concerns will have a significant result on your evaluation of the present numbers and on the projections you'll make regarding the property's future efficiency.

Take a look at the Property Tax Bill.

That's one means to verify the precision of this cost, yet also want to see if the current owner has obtained some type of tax reduction (perhaps a development incentive) that might expire and not apply all to the new owner. Look for proof of a "phase-in" of a new analysis. Some cities, to alleviate the effect that the regular review of property worths can create, will choose to apply a new report in phases. This can mean that the current tax is precise, but there is also the assurance of a higher tax rate as the new evaluation comes online.

Recite the Representations about the Leases and the Schedule of Rent Income in the Offer to Purchase

Check with an attorney about the proper language, however, go into the offer to buy something along the lines of, "The Seller warrants and represents that as of the date of this contract, the leases are for such and such amounts and the expiration dates and renewal options are whatever." Ask the legal representative about adding " and that these guarantees will endure the shipment of the deed." The first part indicates the seller tells nothing but the fact, and the second part implies that she or he is not off the hook if you discover the lie after you finish the purchase. When faced with having their words immortalized like that in a contract, it's amazing how many sellers get religious beliefs.

Rule of Thumbs: Forget the legal representative jokes and get yourself an excellent lawyer. You need someone with knowledge in financial investment property, not necessarily the individual who did your last house closing (single-family closings are to attorneys what oil changes are to car mechanics). A tight purchase contract or a great lease can conserve you money and grief.

Market-Related Data.

Examine Comparable Sales.

If you were pondering the purchase of a house, you would like to know how much other homes in the neighborhood had cost. Sales of comparable properties do not tell you as much about a financial investment property as they do about house sales, but they can sometimes offer useful insight. There are some apparent issues with trying to use raw "compensations" information that you usually from a real estate agent. One problem is merely the absence of enough comparables to be significant. Let's state that you're looking at 10,000 square foot shopping mall. How many recent sales of centres the same size in the same market location are you going to see? Most likely inadequate to supply a significant sample.

Your search may be a bit more efficient if you take a look at some other properties related to these comparables. The total square video is one. You might discover that three-strip centres have sold in the last year, but each was a different size. You might examine the market price per square foot to see if you can recognize a pattern. You might also consider each property's gross rent. Dividing the asking amount by the gross rent gives you something called the total lease multiplier.

Keep in mind, nevertheless, that you are not most likely to find this type of information online without having to spend for it.

If you're dealing with a broker, he or she should be a great source of information. Even before computers made it simple to keep property records, excellent business brokers always built up information about every property they came in contact with. Ask for it.

One last word on comparable sales data as it connects to income-producing property. Remember your mantra: You're genuinely purchasing the income stream. Equivalent sales information are useful insofar as they offer us a feel for your market. Information seldom tells you enough on their own, but to lead you to a decision about selling or buying.

Try To Find Lease Rates and Operating Expense Data.

As you enter serious property analysis and projections, you need to understand what occupants want to pay for area and how much owners are required to pay for operating expenses.

Once again, you can ask the commercial broker to share those details. It would be an excellent idea to relaxing as much as a property manager as well (you may require his services later) because a manager will have very first- hand knowledge of what it truly costs to run a particular kind of property.

Discover Local Capitalization Rates.

Unless you read this book from the back to the front, you might not know yet what a capitalization rate is. Suffice it to say for now that it is among several rate-of-return measurements that you will want to know. For the kind of financial forecasting, you'll learn to operate, it's essential to understand what the regular capitalization rate is for a particular type of property in a specific geographic location. Once again, your industrial broker is the very first person to ask.

Equipped with the self-confidence that you can collect the information you require to do a sensible property analysis, turn your sights now onto some genuine numbers.

Marketing

Before you can put a property in the market, you need to be sure that the market is all set and ripe for it. You should have done a great deal of investigation of the real estate market in the area where your house is before you purchased it, but as soon as your property is ready for assessment, you need to know how the present market is doing. Examine your newspapers to see the prices of houses in the location. Ensure that the discussion of the home is very first-rate. People can be postponed by getting to a property to see trash outside. They want to see a pretty front yard. Ensure the windows are tidy, and that the house is presented naturally.

You might wish to consider leasing furniture to put into the house. Often people are more lured by seeing a home with living areas already set up so they can begin to imagine their use of the building. The idea is that you give your house as a prospective blank canvas, but with enough, in it, for people to be able to consider it as a potential home. If it's cold and does not look that nice, they might not have the ability to see past this, so you do need to dress the house all set for viewings.

You need to focus on the specific market you think your home fits. When the property agent calls, ensure that they have the right information to share with possible purchasers. Marketing the house is essential, and you need to be contented with the photographs. If you are not, take much better ones and ask to change their documents. They will generally be all right with this if you approach it entertainingly.

Choosing the best property agent is essential. You need to understand that the real estate agent has an excellent customer base, a good quality website, plenty of contacts, and the potential to promote your property sufficiently. If you find that one local property company is more prominent than another, then this might be a time to make an option between the two.

You also need to know if you are allowed to advertise yourself. When people enter into flipping houses, typically, they create a site to provide their homes more prominence. However, in the initial stages, your energy would be much better invested in a real estate agent. There might be basic property websites if you can point questions toward them, where you can promote, but it's helpful to work with a real estate agency and ask them. Find out if there are discount rates for the sole company. That means that you leave the property with one agent, and they charge you less. Learn also if they want to give a discount if a potential buyer gets near to the asking cost.

The price at which you market the property needs to be competitive, but it must also be high adequate to ensure that if someone makes an offer, they feel like they are getting a bargain. Add 10 percent to what you'd like to get for the house and hope that someone will offer the price that you want. Make sure that your house is warm and inviting at all times. The presentation is everything. Make sure you ask for feedback so you can make adjustments if something has been spotted that you didn't think about.

Turning a profit on a house need to be possible if you had studied the market before you began the restoration of your home and know what kind of accommodation people want. The house that you purchased might have many rooms, but by turning it into a clear plan, you might likewise bring more people to look at the home. The marketing of the house is essential. You might even wish to have an open house day, but if you do this, make sure that your home is perfect on those days so that people do not just turn around and drive away.

The more welcoming you be, the better. Walk through the house and look for strong points to give ideas to the real estate agent about things you feel will market the place. Make sure all jobs are done and that the potential purchasers have nothing to repairs that will be used as bargaining power when they are making offers.

The Potential of Buying a House Auction.

If you are considering buying a house at auction, you have to know what you are doing. People want quick sales, but there may be reasons behind it other than the apparent. You need to investigate the house thoroughly, but you only have a short time to do it. To make the most of this situation, you need to follow a specific procedure:

Set up your financing

Know from your bank how much you can borrow at short notice and work out your budget the same way you would for buying on a regular sale.

The house is only worth a set price which should consist of:

- The asking price
- The cost of refurbishment
- The potential asking price

If the house costs $200,000 and the potential repairs look like they could come to $90,000, you will need to have $290,000 available to you, but you will also need some kind of assurance that the fully refurbished house could see at more than $290,000 to make a profit.

Because of that, you will also need to be aware of the real estate market in the area where the house is located. Look at similar properties. Ask around. Be mindful of what you are getting yourself into because you don't have time to go back on your word that you will buy the property. You need to know what the house is worth to you.

Inspecting the property

We have already told you in another chapter what to look for when you are buying a property, but bear in mind that when you are buying at auction, you have a limited time to put all your estimates together. If you can take your contractor with you, you may have to pay them a little to give you the time, but it will worth it because they will know what to look for and will be able to provide you with an idea on remedial costings.

If there are questions that you have about the property, make sure that you have asked them before the sales day. They will be dealing with a lot of questions and it's up to you to ask relevant questions. You don't have the same level of control when you buy at auction, so if this means writing things down, do so and make sure that you know what you are buying.

Decide on a set budget

This is vital because it is straightforward to do with bidding. If the home reaches the amount that you have found viable, and there are still bids coming, walk away. You won't make money on the property and it's one of the biggest mistakes that real estate flippers make. They hear others bidding, and they are selling beyond what is reasonable. Then when it comes to renovating the house, they are already working with a shortfall of money, making the budget very tight and may end up taking a loss on the property.

On the auction day

Have a set budget for how much you can spend on the house and do not go beyond it. When the auction is in progress, don't be too keen to get your offers in. Wait and see how the bidding goes so that you know who your competition is. Go in with a bid when you are ready and remember that you have a top budget and stick to it.

You will be expected to pay for the property if you are the champion of the public auction in advance. It will be useful to search for out what costs are entailed when you buy your house, and right before the public auction, you can place this out from asking the personnel at the public auction house. This kind of buying is suitable for those that are cash buyer because they know their precise monetary situation and likewise spot how much cash they have left to do the repair work, of acquisition is appropriate for those that are cash customers. If you do not have some money but have prepared to lend, you have to work your possible revenue much less anything that investing will cost you. You must make sure that the loan provider is gotten ready for early repayment and will certainly not bill you way too much in the way of costs for very early reimbursement.

CHAPTER THREE

Why Do So Many Property Owners Fail?

They started investing in real estate 30 years ago with so much hope for their future.

A rental house here, a duplex there, and soon they had a rental profile that would make anybody proud. They proactively handled their residential or commercial properties and worked to see they were running at peak effectiveness. Several years earlier, the husband and wife both retired from their daily work and relieved into retired life - funded by their rental income and social security.

This year, they are submitting personal bankruptcy and losing a bulk of their homes to repossession.

They began buying real estate 30 years back, with a lot of expectations for their future.

Most of these people, I would guess, will never again be active in real estate investing. They worked hard for years to build a financial future for themselves, only to see it come tragically crashing down around them, dashing any hopes for lasting wealth creation.

This asks the question: why?

Let's consider some of the possible factors rental property capitalists go broke and discover the essential things you can do to secure your real estate investment.

If real estate is a high investment as most of us (on BiggerPockets) make it to be, why do so many investors stop working?.

Maybe perhaps, how do you avoid this opportunity in your own life? This concern has been swimming around in my mind for some time now.

"What is it that establishes effective investors besides those that stop working?" The answers are as diverse as the personalities of the person with whom we've talked about. What is it?.

One will notoriously say, "Everyone's brilliant in a bull market." Is that what real estate is? Do some people just get fortunate while others do not?

Too Much Risk?

Firstly let's discuss the elephant in the room; risk

Risk is essential in every investment. After all, you know the word "more risk, more reward."

But, there is a tipping point at which the risk becomes too much. Perhaps it's overleveraging properties by obtaining too many "low-down" deals that didn't deal after all, or maybe it's trying to buy too many features too fast. Perhaps it's the constant refinancing of the properties, pulling out all the equity and investing it in more deals. Whatever the reason for the bankruptcy, the risk became too much, and these investors lost.

As rock 'n' roller Nick Cave sang, "If you're going to eat with them cannibals, one way or another, beloved, you're going to be consumed.".

How can somebody avoid this? Play it safe, ultimately? Invest in 100% risk-free bargains?

Risk is fundamental in every investment there is. You recognize the expression.

"even more danger, even more benefit".

Let's talk about the elephant in the area: risk. I warn anybody analysis this word, including me, to consider danger as a useful yet hazardous device - and to always remember that this tool cut both ways.

Not Enough Education?

Many people jump into purchasing property before knowing what they are doing. They merely decide that property is the right path for them and start buying properties. There is a big difference between being busy and working, and this holds with a lot of real estate investors; they think that because they are purchasing homes, they are going to succeed. Never mind that they bought the wrong property in the wrong location with the improper funding.

The solution to this problem is the right education.

I'm not discussing the "get rich fast," late-night tv kind of education. I'm talking about taking the time needed to construct an educational foundation that can support your investing future.

Furthermore, I motivate you to continue finding out through

library books, meetups, and other low-priced resources. You don't need to invest millions of dollars for an education. Information has been democratized, so you just need to reach out and get it. No one can do it for you!

Inadequate Analysis?

When I initially started investing in real estate, I thought I understood what I was doing, but I made some huge mistakes since I didn't do a thorough analysis.

You see, a lot of people buy homes without doing the right calculation. As I often say, "Without the right calculation entering into financial investment, you'll never get the right income from it."

The future is impossible to understand, but with reliable analysis, it's much simpler to predict. We'll talk a lot more about analysis throughout this book, and I would encourage you to look at these areas with the respect the subject deserves. Bad calculation produces bad financial investments!

Are You Working On Your Business or In Your Business?

Is real estate your financial investment or your pastime?

I believe one of the most significant factors investors stop working is that they don't treat their business like a business.

They never develop systems to assist them as they grow. They treat their real estate investment like friends.

They do not produce clear policies for finding excellent renters.

They simply approach investing like a church picnic, and it reveals.

If you wish to avoid stopping working, treat your rental property service the same way a CEO would look at any other company, because that is what it is. Monitor your business's health, hire the right individuals to do the right tasks, and always find ways to improve your bottom line to create a long-lasting business.

So Why Do They Fail?

An investor may fail for a range of factors. Nevertheless, in my restricted time on this planet, I've seen the four errors I just listed played out time and time again in the lives of those who eventually stopped working in their investments. It breaks my heart to see somebody so fired up about what property might do only to lose it all in bankruptcy.

Do not be that person.

If you wish to avoid losing all the tough work you are putting in (or all the effort you are about to put in), take note of the following four points:

-Know that risk is a useful but dangerous tool, so walk accurately.

-Build a strong instructional foundation for yourself before getting in unfathomable.

-Do not stint the calculation. Always know the amounts for any property you buy.

-Deal with your business, not in it. Treat your investments like an investment which they are.

Stopping (or Not Quitting) Your Job Through Rental Properties

Let's be sincere: we all dream of stopping our jobs, whether next year or in the coming years. And realty is attractive, like the financial liberty it can use through rental properties. But when is the best time to stop? Do you need to leave your job to become a successful investor? What if you love your job?

Should You Quit?

Do you love your current job? I guess that if you are reading this book, you probably do not. According to Forbes [iii], nearly two-thirds of Americans are not pleased with their work.

Permit me to share some thoughts on how you can quit your unpleasant (or not so unpleasant) job and embark on a career in property investing, whether you are ready to give up in 20 days or 20 years. Keep in mind; it won't be simple. Rental property investing is not a get-rich-quick technique. It takes dedication, perseverance, and perhaps even luck.

Before you put in your two weeks notification, we ought to get a few things straight.

1. Stopping Your Job Soon Through Rental Properties Will Be Hard

You can earn money reasonably quickly in property in a lot of ways, but rental property investing is not one of them. Wealth is integrated into the long term, and as a result, you'll probably not quit your job next week unless you currently have a large quantity of investment capital with which to begin or you wish to make rental property investing a job, which brings me to my second point.

2. Real Estate Investing Can Be a Job or an Investment. Which One Do You Want?

A job is something that makes you money today, to survive on. You put in the hours, and cash is deposited into your checking account. An investment, but is money made from primarily passive sources. House flipping and property wholesaling, for instance, are "jobs." Owning rentals is a financial investment (preferably!).

Which one do you want?

This might appear to be an odd question, and there is no universal right or wrong response, but I think that thinking this one through all the way is virtually essential. You see, there are a lot of other options if you don't like your present job. Entering into full-time property investing needs not to be your only option to a lousy task. Why? Because real estate investing for income is a task. Know that jerk from work you do not like and want to escape? Yep, he'll be to your real estate investing job, too, in some type. Know the pressure you felt at your work to do? Yep, that will be there. The grass is not necessarily greener on the other side.

There is one vital reality that I harp on all the time: Find what you love to do in life more than anything else, and do that for a career. If that means tutor high school math, teach high school mathematics. Find a job that lets you take a trip around the world if that means traveling the world. And if that means investing in real estate for income, then invest in realty for income.

Now let me clarify something crucial here: I'm not recommending that you should just buy real estate if you love buying real estate. If you like investing in real estate, I'm saying you must only invest in real estate as a career. Do you see the subtle difference?

I think everyone can and need to include property investing as part of their plan for retirement and wealth structure. That does not always involve doing it full-time and making a consistent income from it. The purpose of owning rental residential or commercial properties is discovered in the flexibility to make the financial investment what you desire. If you mean "passive," then you can make it (mostly) passive.

CHAPTER FOUR

What Do Successful Investors Really Buy

Do successful investors want properties in the best condition or those that require work? Do they want commercial or residential, city or suburban, brick or frame, or blue or gray?

While any of these choices (other than possibly the color) might fit much better in a specific person's comfort zone, the real financier deals with the physical property as a secondary issue. He or she is not thinking about buying the property but purchasing the property's expected financial benefits—which is called the income stream.

Rule of Thumb: Don't decide to buy, hold, or sell based on psychological aspects. In particular, don't purchase a property because you've fallen in love with it; and do not buy because of a sentimental attachment when you should sell.

To the extent that some quality of the physical property or its surroundings will affect that income stream, then that attribute becomes significant. Will the arrival of a significant new employer bring about an increase in the demand for apartments? This might be the time to look at real estate if so. Would the chance for increased rents more than the expense of renovating a specific property? Possibly you should look for a fixer-upper.

A sensible investor seeks a return on investment. To accomplish that return, she or he has to look at the amount thoroughly-- at the present financial data and at sensible projections of how the investment will perform in the future. As the preceding Rule of Thumb makes clear, no active real estate investor buys a property-- or even worse yet, holds one too long-- because of an emotional attachment to that property. The decision to sell and buy are based on monetary worth, on the income stream, and on the return on investment that the income stream represents.

Start your calculations and principles just as you would if you were constructing a new building. Start with the structure: the four fundamental investment returns.

How You Make Money in Real Estate: The Four Basic Investment Returns

Virtually all the procedures and principles that we will discuss in this book relate to four crucial components that, to a higher or lesser degree, occupy every income-property investment. They are the ways you generate income with rental property. You can call these the four fundamental elements of returns:

1. Cash Flow

2. Appreciation

3. Loan Amortization

4. Tax Shelter

Not every income-property investment will supply these returns in an equal rate. Each is unique and will mix the four benefits differently; some financial investments may even lack one or more. One property may give you an excellent annual capital; another might yield little or no cash from year to year, but provide the potential of a huge payday when you sell. These four returns involve the complete pool of potential benefits. The investment choices you make will depend on your objectives and the strength of these several returns. You're right on your way to success if you know where they come from and how to determine them.

From this point on, nearly every estimation and idea we discuss will relate in some method to these four fundamental returns. Let's look at them extensively.

1. **Cash Flow**

Do you have a checkbook? You already know cash flow, if so. Cash is comes in, money goes out. When you would like to know the balance in your checkbook, it does not matter where the money came from or where it went. All that matters is how much came in and how much goes out.

You're interested exclusively in the circulation of money, for this reason, the name capital. If you look at a specific time (12 months is typically a practical option), you'll need to know if more cash comes in than expenses. If at the end of that year you can say that you took in more money than you spent, then you had a "positive cash circulation" for the year. Another term you will, in some cases, see for positive cash flow is "net spendable cash," which describes the cash flow that is left over after you pay your income taxes on the property's earnings. If a property investment has a positive capital (i.e., if there is money left over after all the costs are paid), that's money, you can remove the table.

On the other hand, if you have spent more than you took in, you had a "negative cash circulation." Nature hates a vacuum (and banks aren't too fond of overdrawn accounts, either), so an unfavorable cash circulation means a shortage that you need to do something about. If you have an adverse cash flow in your checkbook, then you know you need to put money in from some other source, perhaps cost savings. If it's your property investment that experiences the negative cash circulation, then you have to make up the shortfall from funds outside the property account, in this case, your pocket. A property with a negative cash flow does not provide you with any spendable money. On the contrary, it requires that you put more of your funds into the property to cover the difference.

Rule of Thumb: If there was any doubt before, there ought to be none now. It is essential to make the kind of financial forecasts that this book is all about. For a small investor, unfavorable cash flow is not just an accounting entry. It means that, at a specific time, the property will not have enough money to pay its bills. That also means that you, as the investor, will have to put your cash to make up the shortage. The presence of periodic negative cash flow doesn't mean that this is a seriously faulty investment; you may make up the loss in other years or through other "four returns." The ability for unfavorable cash flow, nevertheless, does bring a vital point front and center: If you make your forecasts and evaluate the general investment to be beneficial, you can prepare for the unfavorable money circulation and take it in step. You can get blindsided if you don't make your forecasts

The arithmetic is simple enough:

Cash in minus Cash Out =Money Flow

Example. Let's look at a primary and typical example of cash flow from income property. You own a six-unit building. 2 units rent for $800 per month, 2 for $900, and 2 for $1,000. All units are inhabited, and everyone pays on time. Monthly you make a mortgage payment of $2,800. For the year just ended, you paid $14,100 in property tax, $3,800 for property insurance coverage, $4,200 for upkeep and repair work,

$ 800 for water, and $75 for miscellaneous materials.

Do the calculation:

Money In

(2 800) (2 900) (2 1,000) $5,400 monthly

5,400 12 months $64,800 each year

Overall Cash Inflows $64,800.

Money Out.

Home loan (2,800 12 months) 33,600.

Real Estate Taxes 14,100.

Property Insurance 3,800.

Upkeep and Repairs 4,200.

Water 800.

Various Supplies 75.

Total Cash Outflows 56,575.

Money Flow 8,225.

You have taken in more than you spent, so you have a positive capital. When calculating money flow, you ought to keep in mind also that the source of the cash inflows and outflows doesn't concern you. Inflows might come from the rent, loan earnings, vending machine revenue, or any property-related source. The same applies to outflows. Payments for operating costs, debt decrease, or even building of other rentals represent outflows that reduce your overall capital.

2. **Appreciation**

Every investor wants to see a good cash flow from his or her property because that means the investment is providing some spendable cash each year, every financier hopes to see a good money circulation from his or her property. Not all residential or commercial properties generate meaningful cash flow, nevertheless, and for those that don't, the next most important of the four standard returns is appreciation. Not to be confused with what you want you could get from your teenage kids, appreciation is defined as the growth in value of a property with time.

The formula here is just as simple as that for cash flow:

Future Resale Priceless Original Purchase Price = Appreciation

With capital, we asked if you had a checking account. If you have a savings account, now we'll ask. If you do, you've seen appreciation at work. You put $1 into the account today—interest, an engine of appreciation, causes it to grow over time.

The questions that should enter your mind right away about real estate appreciation are, "How much growth?" and "How long?" To address these questions, you need to consider a more fundamental concern, "What causes a property to appreciate in worth?". In general, nevertheless, income-- particularly net revenue (after working expenditures)-- drives the worth of income property. We're returning to one of our standard concepts here that investors truly purchase the property's income stream. If you have more income streams to sell, you can expect to get more for it. The faster and the greater your revenue increases, the more likely it is that the worth of the property will increase.

So, what makes income increase? Changing market conditions may make the property more attractive. An area that was once marginal become fashionable, and consequently, the balance of supply and demand shifts. General economic inflation may cause the rate of new construction to increase, putting upward pressure on rent.

External forces are not the only aspects that can affect appreciation. You might make physical enhancements to the property so that it can command a higher rent. You might just improve the management of the property, drawing in and keeping better occupants, reducing job losses, and reducing wasteful expenditures.

You might not enjoy the benefit of appreciation now until you sell, but when you sell, the worth of this benefit can be significant. If this were a get-rich-quick book, we would probably be talking about something else.

Example. You purchase a property on January 1, 2006 for $1,000,000 and sell it on June 30, 2010 for $1,450,000. What is the rate of appreciation?

The amount of appreciation is the difference between the market price and your initial purchase price, $1,450,000 less $1,000,000, or $450,000.

Future Resale Price $ 1,450,000 less Purchase Price $ 1,000,000 = Appreciation $ 450,000.

3. **Loan Amortization.**

When somebody else pays your costs, it's amusing. That's what happens when you use a loan amortization to acquire an income property. Think about a $1 million office structure. You might write a check for the total but, regretfully, that would almost clear out your savings account. On the other hand, you might write a check for just $300,000 and get a loan for $ 700,000. That would leave you with enough money to buy two more similar structures and still have change leftover.

A loan needs payments, usually regular monthly. Where will the money come from to make these payments? Remember our earlier cash flow example. The mortgage payment was among the cash outflows, and it was paid with the cash that came in. With most properties, rental income makes up all or nearly all of the cash inflow, so basically, it is your occupants who pay your mortgage.

Each mortgage payment you make includes both interest and principal. You use a mortgage loan to acquire the property. Monthly your renters give you the money required to pay for that financial obligation. They are assistance- ing you buy the property.

Amortization is the liquidation of this financial obligation by the application of installment payments over time.

Debt Service (i.e., total mortgage loan payment) less Interest Paid = Amortization.

You will typically take a look at income-property information on an annualized basis, so you can expect to see the term "annual debt service" (ADS). The ADS on a mortgage is the totality of all payments you make in a year.

Example. You make monthly mortgage payments of $1,500. At the end of the year, your bank reports that you have paid $15,000 interest for the year. What is your loan amortization for the year?

If you pay $1,500 each month, then your ADS is $1,500 times 12, or $ 18,000. You apply the formula:

Annual Debt Service ($ 1,500 12) 18,000 less Interest spent for the year 15,000 = Amortization for the year $ 3,000.

4. Tax Shelter.

The last of the four standard returns is a tax shelter. An income-property investment can shelter some of its income from taxes and sometimes shelter income gotten from other investment sources. How does it do that?

As the owner of an investment property, you take in taxable rental income and payout tax-deductible operating costs like insurance and repairs), leaving you with a "net operating income" (NOI) on which you will be expected to pay taxes. However, to promote the general financial benefits that tend to stream from real estate development (e.g., the development of workplace and retail space, multi-family housing, and so on), the tax code allows further deductions.

The first of these reductions are for home mortgage interest. Interest is genuinely an expense connected with getting the property instead of operating it, and even though your renters seem to pay the interest together with the rest of your mortgage, the IRS allows you to deduct that interest.

The second source of tax shelter is through the depreciation deduction, which is now called expense healing in the tax code;

however, it is still usually called depreciation by real flesh-and-blood investors. Even though the market value of the property is probably increasing with time, you can make the assumption that the structures (but not the land) are wearing out gradually and becoming less relevant. You can take a reduction for that presumed decrease in the worth of your asset. (In case you're tempted to stop checking out today and go out to buy the entire area, it's just fair to alert you that what the IRS giveth, it at least partially taketh away later on when you sell.

The exciting part about depreciation is that, if any part of the tax code can be so explained, is that it is a non-cash deduction. Simply put, you get a deduction without writing a check. It does not affect your cash flow and it is not an operating cost. It is a reduction that can protect some or all of your property's year-to-year income from taxation. If the devaluation reduction is significant enough, it can even exceed the quantity required to shelter the property's income and supply shelter for other investment income also. Because case, the deduction produces what is effectively a cash yield of its own by lowering your other tax liabilities.

To anybody who has ever tried to submit a tax return, it should come as not a surprise that you can not find a great basic formula for the tax shelter part of realty investment. Nevertheless, you can at least get an idea by following this path:

Income less Operating Expenses = Net Operating Income.

Net Operating Income less Mortgage Interest less Depreciation (Cost Recovery) = Taxable Income.

Example. Let's review the property you looked at in the above capital example. You can use the same rental income and running expenses. You have a rental income of $64,800 and operating expenditures of $ 22,975. (Neither the total mortgage payment nor just the interest portion is an operating expense).

Income $ 64,800 less Operating Expenses $ 22,975 = Net Operating Income $ 41,825.

You have to know your loan interest and allowable depreciation to complete the calculation. State that your mortgage interest for the year is $32,000 and your deduction for depreciation is $8,000.

Net Operating Income $ 41,825, less Mortgage Interest32,000, less Depreciation $ 8,000 = Taxable Income $ 1,825.

Recall from the capital example that this property has a positive money circulation of $8,225. You can put $8,225 (less income tax payable) in your pocket, but, you now see that you need to pay taxes on only $1,825. This is excellent. It's a tax shelter at work.

The foundation is now in place. You comprehend that every income property can provide you with as many as four various returns: cash flow, appreciation, loan amortization, and tax shelter. Capital is the money you have left after paying all your costs; gratitude is the growth in equity caused by an increase in the property's worth; amortization represents the development in the capital generated by the progressive paydown of your mortgage, and tax shelter means the property's ability to protect from tax some of its income and possibly income from other financial investments.

From this point on, practically every principle and computation we discuss will bear some relationship to one or more of these four standard returns. You're all set to get serious about real estate investing.

CHAPTER FIVE

Attitude to Investing

Are you thinking about buying real estate? Do you feel inspired by the truth that a lot of the richest people worldwide have collected their wealth through this market? Many people are conscious that real estate investment is one of the few ways that an average Juan Dela Cruz can strike it big without needing to leave the nation as an OFW. Because of this, buying realty has ended up being a popular choice amongst many countries.

Nevertheless, certain things make some people remote to this kind of undertaking. Lack of understanding of the ins and outs of the industry, along with insubstantial investments, are just a few of the many reasons some people keep back from starting this kind of investment.

However, the reality is real estate offers a broad array of opportunities for the beginning investor. Mortgages and loans are available to use monetary assistance to first-time investors. Aside from that, with the best attitude and perseverance, you can study your way into becoming an expert investor. Combine that with years of experience, and you can become a professional in no time.

As a beginner in real estate investors, you need to consider these several alternatives on investment methods and find which of these is most appropriate to your needs and skill.

1. Buy and Sell

Sell and purchase is most likely the most popular way of earning revenues in real estate. In this strategy, you buy a property and then sell it for a higher price. How is this possible? For one, you can let the property wait and sit up until its market price appreciates in time. You can put it out into the market for a more prominent rate tag when it does.

Now, if you want to take instant action, an alternative would be to increase the worth of the property or website through remodelling and enhancement. You can recondition an old home, purchase new furniture, have the walls repainted, and repair the garden yard. After that, the value of your home increases substantially.

Another alternative would be to purchase properties that are listed below market value—examples of such as foreclosures in addition to features that require urgent selling. You can then sell the property at the current market price and make your earnings.

2. Rental Option

In this option, you buy a property such as a house, commercial space, or home, and after that, you rent it out to tenants. The regular monthly rental fee can then be used to pay for the home mortgage you have gotten to acquire the property. When calculating the rental cost, do not forget to include other expenses such as taxes so that you can have a favorable capital.

3. Pre-construction

With the broad expansion of condominium constructions all over the metropolis, purchasing a pre-constructed condo unit has been a popular alternative for many people. Buy property direct from the designer for a lower cost and then market the system on completion for a greater worth. Considering that you can offer the order in cash, you can quickly pay for the loan you have gotten to spend for the system during its pre-selling stage.

4. Real Estate Stocks

If you are the passive type of financier and you do not wish to be exhausted with having to deal with occupants and mortgage payments, you have the alternative to place your investment funds into the stock market through the equities of significant builders and developers.

Property investing is not precisely a new endeavour, a minimum of people who have attempted their luck in this field. If you can find how you can make money in this business, you might be able to quit your 8-5 day job and live a life with a long-lasting income from your investment Properties.

You can get huge money from an investment property. However, that is if you are equipped with the right information, the appropriate mindset, and the earnest will to be successful. Being a new investor can be threatening.

As a first-timer in this industry, it is sensible to discover all the elements of the estate market.

Many people fail to see that skills fade, but properties are permanent.

They don't understand their entire financial education in their lives is totally wrong!

A lot of people believe that a good job, exceptional abilities, and a positive attitude will make them make wealth. The problem is that it just doesn't work that way. People who make an annual salary and an hourly wage can not build wealth. This is because their cash does not work for them, and instead, they work for their money. This concept keeps them from knowing that the only way to create wealth is to purchase multiple incomes that you don't have to work for, but instead build yourself or acquire from someone else.

Another mistaken belief of multiple incomes and passive income is that people assume government and financial organizations offerings such as the stock exchange, CD's, and lots of other financial instruments are passive income. Most times, unless it is a note or bond that pays you regular interest. It is not a real passive income or a stream of income. As a stream of income or passive income is income that you make every day, every month, and every year consistently as cashflow. Stocks and so on only make you money on the sale and nothing in the meantime, which means they are not cashflow. For instance, it is the same as buying a piece of fine art and hoping that it appreciates the longer you hold it, which is dangerous and locks your money up from better uses.

Realty as an Investment

Property is the King when it comes to developing wealth for people. No other investment has the qualities and capabilities like property do. It is always gaining and appreciating value. Because people require a place to live, it is still in demand. And above all, it is a real property that isn't going anywhere soon—enabling you to borrow against it as security and even to write off all expenses and costs associated off on your taxes. Now let's not wait a moment longer to enter into Real Estate as an Investment.

Property You Can Buy as Investments

There are many ways to purchase realty, and the significant distinctions pertain to how much capital you will need to put to buy them. This might be as low as $40,000 -$ 50,000 to purchase an apartment outright, to only $10,000+ to buy a $100,000 single-family house, or to as much as $20,000-$ 30,000 to acquire a multifamily apartment (2-4 units). All of which are Residential and can be quickly financed.

Once you have up to four units, small office complex, and residential or commercial properties, you're going into business area and have a lot more hoops to leap through and need to start dealing with commercial financing, which can require sizable quantities of capital before they will lend. In the rear, a mobile houses and parks, which are hard to sell, but can cashflow in all sorts of incredible ways from borrowing on the mobiles themselves to charging them for leasing making use of the land. All of which is taxed as land, which is the most affordable tax rate you can have on a property.

- **Condos/Flats** - Condos and flats are the best to purchase for cashflow as they give the best cap rates. The only problem that comes on the resale as some can be challenging to finance as an investment property, avoiding a large part of the population from being able to acquire them.

-Single-Family Homes - Single-family houses are easy to rent, simple to sell, and simple to fund.

-Duplexes/Triplexes/Quads - Small multifamily residential or commercial properties (2-4 systems). These property types combine the funding and simple acquiring advantages of a single-family house with the cashflow advantages and less competition discovered in more significant financial investments.

-Small Apartments - Small home structures are made up of between 5-50 systems; they can make considerable cash flow but can be extremely illiquid on the resale.

-Small Commercial Office Space - Buying little business structures and leasing office space to company professionals.

-Industrial Properties- Manufacturing, warehouses, warehouse, and so on

- **Mobile Homes** - Inexpensive way to get in the world of real estate investing and can also experience significant cashflow.

- **Mobile Home Parks** - The whole park in which mobile homes are situated on can likewise be purchased and sold. Rent the person lots to mobile homeowners, and also to have corporately owned and rented ones.

Strategies in Finding Investment Properties

Just as there are a million ways to skin a feline, there are a million ways to find residential or commercial properties for investment, of all the ways to find the property for investment. The most typical methods are to find the owner straight and give them a cash offer, to find homes that are owned by a lender or bank that they want to get rid of at a discount rate or acquire a lien on the property so you can shut out on the property yourself.

-**Lease Options** - Buying the property and "renting" it with the legal right to purchase it later.

-For Sale By Owners (FSBO) - Private owners sell their property themselves with an indication or newspaper ad, they might want to sell their properties at a discount to avoid paying a real estate agent.

-REO's - Foreclosed Property owned by banks can be purchased under the market if the need isn't too high.

-Auction at the Courthouse Steps - During the procedure of foreclosure, a house is brought to the courthouse actions to be sold to the highest bidder.

-Purchasing in Pre-foreclosure - Sellers on the edge of losing their property can be extremely encouraged to sell their property and conserve their credit and their lives.

-Brief Sales - A bank will typically take less than the loan amount on a property to save from the hassle and expenses of foreclosing and reselling.

-Tax Liens - When property owners refuse to pay their taxes, the government can seize and resell the property.

-HUD Foreclosures - When a US government made the sure loan is foreclosed on, it typically becomes the property of the department of Housing and Urban Development.

-VA Foreclosures - Similar to the HUD foreclosures, the United States Department of Veteran's Affairs sells their houses as well after foreclosing on one of their insured properties.

Strategies in Buying, Renting, and Selling Properties:

When you lastly have the property in your grasp, there are lots of ways you can use to optimize your return. Some properties are suitable for buy n' holding. Meaning you purchase them for cash flow but are expecting to also make a sizable return on the resale due to gratitude.

Next is Fixing N' Flip/Hold, which is finding residential or commercial properties underestimate and fixing them correctly either keep for cashflow or to offer immediately for instantaneous earnings. There is Turn-key-Investing; this is where you find the property, turn it into rewarding cash flow, and give it as a source of income to a considerable investment. For Big Commercial, there is NNN leasing that involves having the business renting the property looks after all the trimmings of the property and pays you for leasing the area. Another Buy N' Hold plan that can make good cash is to turn your Buy N' Hold property into a Vacation Rental and charge three times as much than a regular lease. Then there is permanent money financing, where you fund others in their fix n' flips, buy n' holds, or the main residence.

-Buy-N-Hold - Buy real estate, lease it, and keep it till the market is on, and an excellent buyer comes along.

-Fix-N-Hold- Buy below market price, remodel to appreciate, and held till the marketplace improves and sell it.

-Fix-N-Flip - Buy well listed below market value, modernize to market rates, and sell it immediately to get your return.

-Turn-Key-Investing - fix-and-flipper, but offers remodelled homes to out-of-town people seeking an excellent place to keep their money moving.

-NNN Lease - Big Businesses lease the structure and pay all expenses connected with the building such as upkeep, taxes, insurance, and more. We can own these buildings for highly-passive income.

-Holiday Rentals - Buying expedition property and leasing it out off and on season (Snowbirds).

-Cash Purchase, Sell on Contract - Buy residential or commercial properties and instantly re-sell them to purchasers who may not be able to qualify for a home mortgage conventionally. When using this method, gather a sizeable down payment.

How to Finance:

Financing is readily offered to anyone who has cash for a deposit. Below are the significant methods you can finance your Real Estate Investments;

- **All Cash** - Property without any mortgage attached is exceptionally stable and a safe return. Might not be as fantastic as when using leverage (like a mortgage).
- **Seller Financing** - Seller owns a property free-and-clear (no loan) and can be worked out with to discover a finance offer.
- **Unconventional Lending** - There are lots of lending institutions that will lend on any deal you have as long as the amount makes sense; this can be anything from landlord loans, had money, and much more.
- **Self-Directed IRA** - If you have a 401(k), throw it out, it's time to put that money in a self-directed IRA and make that money lastly work for you than expecting some money manager who is just trying not to lose your money than make you any. You can use your cash in your SD-IRA to do all the plans of buying, selling, and leasing.

- **20% -25% Down Conventional Investment Mortgage** - buy a realty investment through a bank. Come up with a 20-25% deposit and have the bank financing the rest.
- **10% HomePath Investment Mortgage**- These types of loan are just readily available on Fannie-Mae backed bank REOs, but can allow a financier to purchase the home for only 10% deposit with other advantages.
- **House Equity Line of Credit (HELOC)** - With considerable equity in the property, M&T can obtain a credit line off M&T Real Estate equity.
- **Small Company Loans** - Banks typically will fund a line of credit or loan for small companies which consist of a real estate investment business.

Most people are active participants of Real Estate Investing because they wish to take control of their lives, and they think that the level of control they want can not be acquired by working for somebody else. Mainly, they wish to take control of their income and time. They don't want to have to rely on strictly one salary, an income source that is controlled by their governing employer. They have a natural desire for several income sources. Realty Investing is a chance for them to use that genuine desire to attain and obtain a diversified income stream.

In other words, they want monetary self-reliance, independence that, they think, will equate to other essential places of their lives. Whether to just have a stable income through being a property manager, or achieving a wealthy status as a realty magnate, it looks apparent that the keys to success lay in finding out all there is to find out about realty investing, and attaining person habits and a robust mental approach that will gain genuine rewards.

Secure individual practices are being arranged, setting objectives, and improving your psychological attitude: having a more positive attitude about your possibilities in life. Also, practical undertakings such as enhancing your credit history through paying off your debts will put you in great shape to be successful at property investing.

Being an investor means ending up being a business owner, an individual who wants to take some risks, an individual who is not going to be in a non-fulfilling but safe task. Taking dangers is always about conquering worries. There are different levels of risks, and fears-usually, an increase in the level of one will increase the level of the other. Going outsides to your car on any particular day will not cause much fear because the risk is not that high. You may get hit on the head by a piano, but that possibility is rather low.

Fears about real estate investing can be relieved by thoroughly studying real estate investing, and discovering the suitable methods for the job.

When you look closely, an investment in real estate is less risky than other financial investments, such as investing in the stock exchange. Several variables impact the stock exchange: political chaos, the weather condition, the change in the cost of products such as oil. A parcel of property, nevertheless, appreciates typically in worth with time, making it a substantial investment. Of course, the profit margin will differ according to the ability, understanding, and experience of the investor and the kind of investor he/she is: such as a property manager or a house flipper.

With the best method, habits, understanding, and fundamental determination, real estate investing might be the right alternative to lots of people. Although, when defined as a "get rich scheme," it might not work too well, it is possible to prosper from real estate investing. The advantages surpass the risks by a substantial margin.

How to Become a Successful Real Estate Investor

The first important step to your success as an investor begins with you. The question - "What is the best mindset that you should have to invest in real estate?" What I get is - decision, imagination, can do, not taking no for an answer, or wanting to succeed at all costs. Those responses all address practically the same belief, and somebody must have a can-do decision, but more is needed.

"Real estate is a service, and if you buy real estate, you are a little businessperson. You hire professionals, you market your items, you spend money on materials, you must keep good records, and you pay taxes on your incomes." Now the rational development of your newfound understanding is that all successful organizations have some things in common; a composed company plan is among those things."

Let's take a look at a business we are all familiar with, GM. When the federal government loaned GM money before their bankruptcy, the federal government required that GM had a possible way to pay back their cash. GM needed to come up with a service plan that made the federal government feel comfortable that they would be paid back.

As an investor in property, the first thing you need to do is understand that you are a small business owner. That understanding brings you disadvantages and prospects.

Your written service plan will assist you in determining what those shortcomings and opportunities are. Your strategy must be noted. Your plan needs to be realistic; it ought to have goals, a schedule, and a budget plan. And, it ought to be done using expert assistance from a competent and expert in the service.

A strategic real estate investment plan is not a pointless document. It is your roadway map to success. It assists you to get going in business now, not later on. It assays your resources; it outlines a course of action; it keeps you focused and on track, and it allows you to assess your efforts.

Making an effort to finish a tactical property investment strategy belongs to the "right" mindset that you need to employ for success. Just the natural act of writing out your plan makes you most likely to be successful than people who don't.

Attitude is not practically a decision, but it's likewise about working smarter, and it's about listening to and taking the guidance of successful others. Belief is about planning for success. If you prepare thoroughly and execute your plan, you will succeed.

Understand that you are a small businessperson, and companies in America get favorable tax treatment. Benefit from that beneficial tax status. Finishing a tactical property investment strategy will assist you to do that.

CHAPTER SIX

Real Estate Opportunities and How to Estimate What an Income Property is Worth

Whether you're a buyer, a seller, or a mortgage lending institution, among one of the essential questions you need to respond to is, "What is this property actually worth?" It might be said that worth, like beauty, is in the eye of the beholder. This disagreement tends to prove out to single-family houses, where standard knowledge has always held that property deserves what somebody wants to invest for it. The income-producing property, nevertheless, is different. The numbers determine value. Let's start this conversation with a topic that regularly heats your heart:

Income.

Everybody in business or finance has run into the term "net income" and comprehends its fundamental significance (i.e., what is left over after costs are subtracted from earnings). When it comes to investment real estate, however- the emergency room, the term internet operating income (NOI) stands for a small variant on this theme and has an exceptionally satisfying significance. You may think about NOI as some of the bucks a property returns in a provided year if the property is acquired for all cash and if there is no reason to consider income tax or devaluation.

By even more official interpretation, it is a property's gross operating income, much less the amount of all business expenses.

Let's assess them briefly:

- **Gross is running income**: Definitions resemble artichokes. You need to peel off the layers off personally. In this instance, start with the gross scheduled income, which is the property's yearly income if all rooms are in indeed rented and all the rental fees collected. Deduct from this amount a share for job and credit rating loss. The outcome is the gross operating income.

Gross Operating Income less Vacancy and Credit Loss =Gross Operating Income

- **Operating expenditures**: This is the term that creates the best mischievousness.

Lots of people say, "If I need to pay it, after that, it's an operating budget." That is not always real. To be taken into consideration a real estate general expenses, a product needs to be needed to preserve an item of a property and to guarantee its ability to remain to create income. Loan payments, depreciation, and capital investment are not considered operating expenses.

For instance, Utilities, products, snow removal, and property management are all operating costs. Repair work and upkeep are operating expenditures, but enhancements and improvements are not-- they are capital investments.

The real estate tax is an overhead, yet your income tax responsibility created by owning the property is not.

Your mortgage interest might be an insurance deductible cost, but it is not an operating budget. You might need a mortgage to manage the property, but not to run it.

Deduct the business expenses from the gross operating income, and you have the NOI.

Gross Operating Income less Operating Expenses = Net Operating Income.

Why the busy? Because NOI is vital to your knowledge of the market worth of a piece of income-producing property. That market value is a function of the property's "income stream," and NOI is at the core of that income stream. As unsympathetic as it might sound, property investment is not a good-looking assemblage of bricks, boards, bx cables, and bathroom fixtures. It is an income stream produced by the operation of the property, free of external elements such as funding and income taxes.

Investors don't decide to purchase properties; they choose to buy the income streams of the homes. This is not such a radical notion. When was the last time you selected a stock based on the looks of the stock certificate? No. You buy the expected financial advantages. The same is true of investors in income-producing real estate.

Those readers who lured to sleep by this conversation will attentively mention that they have observed changes in the value of income property brought about by changes in mortgage rates of interest and tax laws. Does not that observation oppose our assertion about external factors?

If you're familiar with the principle of capitalization rate (which we'll go over again below), you acknowledge that there are two components to a property's worth formula: the NOI and the cap rate (universal shorthand for capitalization rate). The NOI represents a return on the purchase cost of the property, and the cap rate is the rate of that return. A property with a $1,000,000 purchase rate and a $100,000 NOI has a 10% capitalization rate. The investor will purchase that property for $1,000,000 just if he or she judges 10% to be a satisfactory rate of return.

What happens if interest rates increase? Because case, there may be other chances competing for the investor's capital-- bonds, for example-- which financier might now have an interest in this same piece of real estate only if its return is higher, say 12%. Use the 12% cap rate (PV NOI/ Cap Rate), and now the investor wants to pay about $833,000. External situations have not affected the operation of the property or the NOI. They have impacted the rate of return-- the so-called market cap rate-- that the buyer will demand, and it is that change that affects the market worth of the property.

In other words, the NOI expresses an objective step of a property's income stream. At the same time, the needed capitalization rate is the financier's subjective estimate of how well his or her capital should do. The previous is primarily science, based on meaning and formula, while the latter is largely art, impacted by elements outside the property, such as market conditions and federal tax policies. The two work together to give you your quote of market worth.

Cash Flow and Taxable Income

So far, our discussion has concentrated on the significance of NOI-- what it includes, what it does not include, and what significance it needs to your understanding of the worth of an income property. As number 1 programs, the subjects of money flow and gross income are natural extensions of NOI.

Net Operating Income

1. Taxable income and cash flow

-- Interest Paid

-- Debt Service

-- Depreciation and Amortization

-- Capital Expenditures

+ Interest Earned + Interest Earned

Taxable Income or Loss Cash Flow before Taxes

When you look back at a year of operating your property, a reasonable question for you to ask is, "How much did I make this year?" The answer lies in an evaluation of the property's cash flow and taxable income.

NOI is the starting point of our conversation here. Once you know the property's NOI, you branch off in one direction to figure its taxable income and in another to calculate its capital.

As you'll see now, these two branches ultimately reconnect to give you your real bottom line. Let's look at these two branches to see how they differ.

Taxable Income or Loss

Both branches start with NOI. Bear in mind that mortgage payments play no part in the NOI calculation, so it is now, below the NOI line, that you will at last take financing into account.

You can subtract the substantial part of the loan payments when you do your taxable income estimation. If you earn interest (on your escrow account, for example), you need to add that back into your income.

You also make deductions for depreciation and amortization. You can't just subtract its full expense as an investment cost when you purchase a piece of real estate investment. Instead, you can deduct each year a part of the value of the depreciable possession, up until finally you have written off the entire amount. With realty, you are allowed to deal with the physical structures (i.e., the buildings) as the depreciable possession for tax functions, however not the land.

(An editorial aside: The author, having found out the industrial real estate company in the Pleistocene Age, still uses the general term, "devaluation." In the Modern Age of unrelenting political accuracy, you will frequently discover this same concept referred to as "cost recovery." Congress, ever the subtle wit, no doubt became unpleasant with an economic term that conveyed the idea of continuous decay and collapse and chosen to change it with one that communicated a sense of a rise-from-the-ashes return to health and wealth. No political program here, of course. It is interesting to note that they might not let go of the term "depreciation recapture," which appears to summon subliminal pictures of the taxpayer as gotten away convict, once again trapped.).

At this writing, you can diminish a domestic income property over 27.5 years, and a nonresidential property over 39 years. Because not everybody sells or purchases on the first of the month, the tax code tries to even matter out with a so-called "half-month convention," which permits the taxpayer to claim only half the regular amount of depreciation in the month that the property is positioned in service, and a half in the month when it is sold. The authors of the tax code could have made matters more precise by just asking you to prorate your partial month of depreciation, just as your bank does with per diem mortgage interest when you buy or sell. However, they didn't.

Another product that affects your taxable income is amortization. It is essential to know that the term, as used here, does not describe the primary portion of a loan payment. Instead, it refers to the procedure of taking a partial yearly tax reduction for an item you are not permitted to expense in a single year. An excellent example of an expense that must be amortized is the premium you pay for securing a loan, typically called "points." You usually pay this premium in one lump sum on the day you close the loan; however, you must amortize it over the life of the loan. If you take out a 240- month investment-property loan for $720,000 that needs payment of two points (2%, or $14,400), you can subtract $60 per month or $720 for each full tax year.

You might also earn some interest income on your property checking account or an escrow account that your lender may need real estate taxes and insurance.

To estimate your taxable income is your NOI less interest payments, less your allowed write-offs for devaluation and amortization, plus any interest made.

2. Net Operating Income.

Taxable income or loss.

-- Interest Paid.

-- Depreciation and Amortization.

+ Interest Earned.

Taxable Income or Loss.

Cash Flow before Taxes.

Capital is even more straightforward, consider it as your property's checkbook. It is all that can be found in, less whatever that goes out. By starting with NOI, you have currently represented all of the lease income, credit losses, and operating costs. Where else do you spend or receive money?

You make mortgage payments, and now you can count the entire payment amount. You may also make capital improvements on property. An improvement extends the life of a property. It's different from a repair, which keeps, instead of boosts, the life span. The expense of the improvement affects your cash flow as soon as you spend the cash, although you may generally have to write it off over 27.5 or 39 years.

Again here, you may make interest income on your property savings account, which also contributes to your cash inflows.

The short version of our discussion now boils down to this: To derive your property's taxable income, you take its NOI, subtract whatever that is appropriately tax-deductible, and add any nonrental income such as interest. To determine its capital, you accept its NOI and deduct everything that was invested but not already represented in the NOI calculation itself.

Once again, add any nonrental invoices.

3. Capital before taxes.

Net Operating Income

-- Debt Service

-- Capital Expenditures

+ Interest Earned

Capital before Taxes

Capital and taxable income are closely related, but still have important distinctions. Cash flow is real. Cash can be comes in;

money goes out. You earnestly hope the difference will always be a positive number, and if it is, you can take it with you; you can invest it.

With all due respect to the substantial industry that is constructed around tax preparation and preparation, gross income is not quite so real. It's whatever the tax code du jour says it is.

If tomorrow your house of Representatives decide that the useful life of an industrial property should be 100 years instead of 39, then your property's taxable income will rise without your experiencing a single additional dollar in rental income. Why? Because the more extended write-off period would mean smaller sized annual reductions for devaluation, and less deductions mean higher taxable income-- even though your gross and net earnings remain unchanged.

Also, if mortgage interest were no longer deductible, the effect of the mortgage payment on your cash flow would remain the same, but the result of the lost reduction would be to increase your taxable income and, hence, your taxes.

Cash Flow after Taxes

We have been talking about cash circulation before taxes (CFBT), but a more significant bottom line to you as an investor might be capital after taxes (CFAT).

Taxable Income or Loss Cash Flow before Taxes

Tax Bracket

Income Tax-- Income Tax

4. Cash flow after taxes.

Capital after Taxes

While taxable income is a somewhat false notion, the tax liability it provokes feels extremely real certainly. Taxable income produces one last money flow item: income tax, which needs to be deducted from your CFBT to give you your bottom line, CFAT.

Once again, recall our discussion above on the four ways to generate income in real estate. Your taxable income may be unfavorable or favorable. If it is negative, then it may lead to adverse tax liability and can increase your CFAT by safeguarding other profits.

How to Analyze a Rental Property

I look at several main factors when evaluating a rental property; however, the two most important are as follows:

1) **cash flow**
2) **appreciation**

Capital is just the cash that's left after all the costs have been paid.

Appreciation is the equity got as the property value increases. As we went over briefly above, there are not a lot of terrific methods to approximate future appreciation without a crystal ball, so I usually choose to focus on the capital. After all, I am a buy-and-hold investor, and I believe any appreciation is "icing on the cake" rather than the objective.

What Is Cash Flow?

As I discussed previously, cash flow is the cash left over after all the bills on a property have been paid. This is an easy enough definition, but it gets a lot of people in problem. You see, technically, capital is defined in this manner: Income - Expenses = Cash Flow

Okay, excellent. However, where people tend to screw things up is understanding what is involved under "income" and "expenses." This difference can get you into a lot of trouble, especially if you forget to note a few of the expenses. Let's look at each one in detail, starting with income.

Computing Income

A property's projected income might look relatively simple to calculate, but provided that all the estimations for capital are based on this number and that the future success or failure of your investment is based on this.

The key to calculating income is knowing the reasonable market rent. The fair market rent is the rate someone wants to pay to use your property for a set time. Fair market lease is determined by the market and what the local average is for specific characteristics of the property, such as the following:

- Location of the property
- Number of bedrooms and restrooms
- Amenities such as air conditioning, parking, and appliances
- Size of the property

When you are choosing how much a property needs to lease for, each of these items comes into play. It's your task, as a property manager, to precisely approximate the potential lease for any property you are managing. This is not always an easy task, but here are several tips for determining what your prospective property might rent for. The following eight tips can be used in determining the rent of a property:

1. **Continuously scan your local documents.** I say "papers," plural because lots of markets are served by more than one. It may appear old-fashioned, but a lot of property owners and tenants are outdated.

2. Inspect out Craigslist typically. Many big and little property owners advertise their properties here, and you can get more info than from the papers. This is a fantastic resource for almost every part of the county. And, you can do keyword searches for your particular market and type of property.

3. Check out your competitors' and local property management business' websites. They will frequently have many listings near you and will show all the facilities.

4. Check out regional "For Rent" signs. Call the number on the signs and act as a potential occupant. This is a fantastic method to learn what houses in your location are rent for.

5. Talk with other landlords. You can find them at your local REIA (Real Estate Investors Association) conferences. Rent is not a huge secret, and if a property owner could increase their rent, they are typically proud about it.

6. When your system goes uninhabited, try to bump up the rent. If the market bears the increased cost, see. If you do not get any takers in a week or so, start getting rid of the price until the system rent. You will eventually discover the market rate.

7. A lot of applicants? Increase the rent. Conversely, if you have many applicants on the first day of availability, your rent is likely too low. Renters flock to an offer. Back up, do a little research, and set the rate higher.

8. Examine the MLS. Many proprietors and realty agents now also note their readily available rental on the local MLS. You should check out this searchable database if you are an agent. If not, you might want to find one to help you.

Once you have quite an excellent idea of what the property will rent for, you need to approximate the expenses of your rental property.

What Every Investor Needs to Know About Cash Flow: Calculating today Value

You'll remember that we discussed earlier, "The Four Ways to Make Money in Real Estate," was capital. Usually, you are happy when more money comes in than heads out. Nevertheless, the cash flow from an income-property investment does not all come all of a sudden, in a single rush. You wish to have positive money flow each year that you operate the property market, but that capital will be higher some years than in others. When you ultimately sell the property, you'll think about the earnings to be part of your overall cash flow for the sale year.

The time worth of money plays an important role when you think about how valuable your property's income streams are. Timing is everything. The money you receive faster is better than the money you get later because the sooner you have it, the quicker you can put it to earn more cash.

You want to compute the PV of those cash flows when you look at the cash flows from a real estate investment. Essentially, this computation provides the same scenario you saw in the previous compound interest example, except you are reading it from the other end of the telescope. Instead of appreciating the smaller worth get bigger, you watch the bigger value get smaller.

You are finding what it is worth right now in today's dollars when you discover the PV of future cash circulation. You are learning the present worth of each of them and then totaling to those specific PVs when you find the PV of a series of cash circulations. The amount of the PVs of each future private capital is the PV of the entire stream of future income.

CHAPTER SEVEN

Property Management

Property management company charges a percentage of the lease typically, in addition to a fee, to rent a system. This amount can differ based on location, but in my area, property managers charge 10% of the monthly rent and 50% of the first month's lease when a system is turned over. Instead of spending the time to get the precise expense of the property management based on the situation rate, I will usually just add 1% to whatever the monthly portion is. In this case, the property supervisor charges 10%, so I'll call it 11%, assuming that an additional 1% will cover the cost of their fee on tenant turnover.

Now, what if you are going to manage yourself? You need to still budget for management. Here's why: if you are capable (and you will be!), you can not handle forever. There will come a day when you will have a lot of residential or commercial properties, and you'll need to start using property management. What takes place if you never budgeted for it? That's right: you lose all your cash flow. So whether you ready to handle yourself or not, budget for a property manager.

Putting All the Numbers Together

At this moment, you ought to have a list of all the expenditures and income sources for your property.

Let's take a look at a theoretical circumstance: 123 Main Street is for sale for $100,000. It is a three-bedroom house that would rent for $1,200 per month.

Breaking down the numbers, we've identified the following monthly costs:

- Taxes - $120/month.
- Insurance - $55/month.
- Flood insurance coverage (if required) - None required.
- Vacancy - 5% or $50/month.
- Repair work - 5% or $50/month.
- Capital expenditures - $183/month.
- Water - Tenant pays.
- Drain - Tenant pays.
- Trash - Tenant pays.
- Gas - Tenant pays.

- Electrical power - Tenant pays.
- HOA charges (if applicable) - None.
- Snow removal - Tenant pays.
- Yard care - Tenant pays.
- Property management-11% or $132/month.

We now understand that our regular monthly costs will balance $590. This number is called our "operating costs." Keep this in mind-- it will be useful soon.

We are not yet done determining our cash flow. There is still one significant expense we have not included: the mortgage!

To determine the mortgage amount, just use an online calculator to identify your regular monthly payment. In our example here, we know the overall expense of the property is $100,000, so our loan amount will depend on how much deposit we put. Let's assume we put 20% down: $100,000 x. 20 = $20,000. Our loan sum would be $80,000 (because $100,000 minus $20,000 is $80,000).

Now we just enter $80,000 into the mortgage calculator to identify our loan payment. The calculator will also ask for an interest rate and loan duration. To figure out the rate of interest, ask a local loan lending institution what current prices are for the kind of property you are trying to purchase. The majority of residential loans (one to four units) will allow you to choose 30 years, whereas the majority of the business property will enable 20-- 25 years. Plug those numbers into the calculator to determine your mortgage payment.

In this case, we'll use an interest rate of 5.5%, and the loan duration of 30 years to discover our monthly payment will be $454.23.

Finally, we have all the pieces needed to create our cash flow analysis problem. We learned previously that our overall business expenses were $590.00 per month, and now we understand our home mortgage will be $454.23. Let's add them together: $590.00 + $454.23 = $1,044.23.

We can approximate that the overall costs on this property will be $ 1,044.23 each month.

Identifying Cash Flow.

Now, let's go back to the meaning of "cash flow" that we discussed previously, which was this:

Income - Expenses = Cash Flow.

We know the overall income, and we know the total expenses, so now we can determine our cash circulation. An example, in this case, our property will rent for $1,200 each month $ 1,200.00 - $1,044.23 = $155.77.

On this sample property, our estimated cash circulation will be $155.77 each month or $ 1,869.24 each year.

Is this a bargain? The cash flow of $155.77 might look like a fantastic offer, or it might look terrible. For that, we need to t look at the return on investment.

Cash-On-Cash Return on Investment.

At this point, we know that our example property will offer us about $155.77 monthly in favorable cash circulation.

This looks good, but is it true?

The best way to determine whether this is a great deal is by comparing it with something else. After all, this investment did cost you cash to buy it, right? You spent $20,000 on the down payment, plus (let's say) another $5,000 on the closing expenses and another $3,000 on repair to get the property 100% rent ready.

At this point, you have paid $28,000 of your hard-earned cash to get the property. So, is $155.77 per month an outstanding deal on a $28,000 investment?

This is when the cash-on-cash return on investment is available at convenient. The cash-on-cash return on investment (frequently abbreviated as CoCROI) is an essential metric that tells us what kind of return our cash is bringing based merely on the cash flow (ignoring appreciation, tax benefits, and the loan paydown). The CoCROI is good because it enables us to compare this investment against other financial investments, like the stock exchange or mutual funds. So let's do that.

CoCROI is just the ratio between how much capital we got over one year and how much money we invested. Just put.

CoCROI = Total Annual Cash Flow/ Total Investment.

So using our example, we get:

CoCROI = $1,869.24/$ 28,000.00 = 6.7%.

We have figured out that this property needs to produce a CoCROI of 6.7%. Is this good? That's up to you to decide. Over the past two decades, the stock exchange has averaged around 7%, so I like to believe 6.7% is a bit listed below typical compared with that, and it's not something I would pursue. Keep in mind; this doesn't take into account the appreciation that will take place, the tax advantages you may receive, or the loan pay down that is taking place (after all, every month, the loan gets paid down more!). The bottom line is: only you can determine what a "good" return on investment is because it will be based on your interpretation of what acceptable is. The question is this: do the property, and its return on investment fits within your plan? You might want to pursue it if so!

What About the Rules of Thumb?

Around the investing world, there are some "guidelines" to help people examine properties a bit better. Wikipedia defines "rule" as "a concept with broad application that is not intended to be strictly accurate or reliable for every single situation. It is an easily learned and quickly used treatment for approximately determining or recalling some value, or for making some decision."

Take note of two aspects of this definition:

1. Not meant to be strictly accurate.

2. Easily learned and quickly applied.

I am cautious to even add this area because of product one but have decided to do so because of aspect 2. You see, I might point out one of the following guidelines with many disclaimers and warnings, but some readers will still lock on to these guidelines as though I were buying for the Ten Commandments! Please comprehend that these are just quick guides, and they are essential for you to be familiar with; they do not bring immense weight in acquiring a property. Their primary function is in helping you to identify harmful properties, so you do not waste time examining them. When you are looking for a genuine estate offer, you will likely have hundreds to choose from. You wouldn't leave your desk if you tried to analyze the income and expenses for each property that comes on your computer screen! Instead, the guidelines are a sort of "internal gauge" that will assist you in identifying whether a property should have further factors to consider.

However, let me get to the two most standard rules, and this will be more clear.

- **The 50% Rule.**

Lots of people are bad at approximating expenses on a possible offer. I just spent a significant portion of this book shows you how to estimate capital accurately, but once again, it would be a waste of your time to do this on every property you come across. For that reason, another, much faster way to estimate cash flow is by using a strategy referred to as the 50% rule. This rule states that a rental property's expenditures tend to be about 50% of the income, not including the loan principal and interest (P&I) payment. The formula looks like this: Cash Flow = (Total Income x. 5) - Mortgage P&I.

Simply put, merely divide the income in half and subtract the mortgage payment!

You were scanning through Zillow.com for properties and came across a duplex that piqued your interest. Knowing the rental rates in the area, you know that the property might rent for $600 per side, for a total income of $ 1,200 per month. You likewise see that the property is being cost $120,000, so you do a quick computation in your head and assume your mortgage payment (without taxes and insurance) would be roughly $550 per month (or just use an online loan calculator to identify this number): Therefore, according to the 50% guideline;

Cash Flow = ($ 1,200 x. 5) - $550.

Capital = ($ 600) - $550.

Money Flow = $50.

In this example, we discover using the 50% guideline that you might expect $50 each month in the capital.

How accurate is this?

It depends. You see, the expenses on this property could differ immensely. The following are usually included in that 50%:

-Taxes Insurance Maintenance Repairs Vacancy CapEx. Property Management.

But what if the taxes were much higher than usual on this property? What if the insurance was higher? Or what if the property was old and for that reason needed lots of continuous maintenance? You see, the 50% guideline doesn't know the details of your property, so it might not be best. It is just a rule of thumb to help you quickly screen homes. Your property's business expenses might be as low as 30% or as high as 70%--you will not know till you run the numbers, however, while you are rapidly taking a look at a lot of properties, the 50% rule can be a great tool to quickly say, "No, no, no, no, perhaps, no, maybe, no, no" on the properties you see. Then you can take a more in-depth look at the "possibly" properties and neglect many of the "no" houses.

- **The 2% Rule (The 2% Test).**

The 2% guideline also helps you evaluate a property for its money circulation capacity, but in a different way than the 50% rule does, because the 2% rule does not approximate how much cash flow you'll receive, but instead acts as a "pass-fail" test to flag properties that call for more analysis.

The 2% rule is simply the ratio between rental income and purchase rate. "Meeting the 2% rule" means that a property's regular monthly rental income needs to equal 2% of the purchase price or more. The formula would look like this: Monthly Rental Income/ Purchase Price = X.

If X >.02, then the 2% rule has been met.

If X <.02, then the 2% rule has not been achieved.

The 2% rule is a dreadful name for this process; it likely has to be called the "2% test." The 2% test, the 2% guideline, is now the 2% test!

Now, the worth of 2% could easily be replaced with another number to check that also. Lots of people look for "the 1% guideline test," in which the regular monthly rental cost is 1% of the purchase rate or more. (Again, it's truly the "1% rule test.")

You may hear people talking about the 5% rule test, the 1.5% rule test, the 3% guideline test. It's all the same thing: the regular monthly lease over the purchase rate.

What does this even mean?

Why does 2% even matter?

What do you win if you "pass the 2% rule test"? A new car? A 40-pound packed animal from the carnival? Barely passing the 2% rule test doesn't imply anything generally.

The 2% rule test is useful once you know your local market. For example, in my regional realty market, I know that if I can find a property that gets to 2%, it's probably going to cash flow well. I know that because the rental income is so high compared with what typical expenses are, it must do pretty well. At the same time, I know that if something falls below 1.5%, it's probably not going to cash flow unless the occupant pays the majority of the expenses. I know for a practically outright reality that it will not cash flow in my area when I get down to 1%!

Now keep in mind that this is my area. Yours might be different. Possibly you'll find that 1% is much to get you enough capital to produce a solid return on investment. The thing is this: do not get trapped on the idea that you have to strike some mythical 2% to have a good investment.

Self-Management Versus Property Management.

When you possess a rental property, should you handle the property on your own or employ an expert to handle it for you? The answer to this question, I'm scared, is plenty "there is no appropriate answer, yet there might be an appropriate response for you." Everyone has various abilities, personalities, and time accessibility. The objective of this area is to help you make the most effective option for you and your family.

Duty of a Property Manager.

Let's address what a property manager does, though. It's challenging to give a straight answer about it! You see, property managers do a broad range of jobs depending on the manager and the owner with whom they are functioning.

Most time, a property manager will certainly be accountable for the following:

Marketing uninhabited devices.

-Evaluating candidates.

-Authorizing occupants and authorizing leases.

-Dealing with calls from occupants.

-Setting up maintenance-related visits.

-Issuing late notifications.

-Declaring expulsions, if required.

-Maintaining a document of income and costs.

-They might additionally pay your property's expenses, depending on the manager.

A property administration business has the framework in position to manage your leasing, consisting of office signs, documents, and team.

Aside from that, property managers use many advantages, such as the following:

They can improve your day, enabling you to invest even more time with friends and family, or at your daily job.

A property manager will certainly have a trustworthy collection of service providers with whom to work and can gain from quantity amounts.

A property manager will certainly have a lead system in position for drawing in prospective lessees. People will know their name, recognize their indications, and call them without their present to market your property.

A property manager can give you even more time to search for various other offers, assisting you to concentrate specifically on the job that generates more income for you.

Strength originates from difficulty, as you believe, you have no doubt found in any area of your life. Problems will emerge, and how you handle them is what specifies your future. In this chapter, I will discover the several difficulties you will come across in your rental property service, particularly on the management of tenants. Troubles will certainly happen in your business, but how you conquer those problems will eventually cause your long-term success. Let's start by talking about one of the most typical issues you'll experience: maintenance and repair.

Repair and maintenance.

As much as I want rental properties to stay in good form permanently, this is not just the case. One of your most vital responsibilities as a landlord is to maintain the property and repair things. This can be demanding and costly; if you followed the analysis part of this book, you would have cash set apart to deal with these issues. Otherwise, you'll have to come up with the cost from your pocket. In either case, the repair service should be done.

The Most Common Repairs You'll Encounter.

One of the most typical repair service demands than can be received from occupants are the following:

1. Fridge/Stove/Dishwasher Not Working - Appliances have a lot of moving parts and, for that reason, tend to break down relatively often. Although some problems can be repaired by the property owner themselves (replacing a burned-out light bulb, setting up a new heating element), several issues will require an expert device repair person. Unless a new device is needed, the reasonable cost to repair this kind of repair is between $50 and $100 per hour, and the majority of repair work can be managed in one hour.

2. Water Leak in Ceiling or Under Windows - Water might be essential for the human body to survive, but it's fatal to a property. If left unchecked, water can ruin wood, drywall, floor covering, and virtually every other surface of your property. Even in small amounts, wetness can cause mold to grow, which can be costly to repair if it gets out of control. When your tenant reports a water problem, make this your number one concern! Work with a certified specialist to check the issue out and repair it immediately. When you're dealing with a water leak, don't work with the cheapest person, hire the best. It's also an excellent idea to know whether your property has water supply lines in the ceiling, so if there is a leak, you can call a plumbing professional instead of a roofing professional.

3. Water Leak Under Sink - A water leakage under a kitchen or restroom sink can have one of two causes: the supply line (the pipeline that brings water to the sink, both cold and hot) or the drain (the drain that takes the water from the sink and sends it out to the pipe). I estimate that 90% of water leakages are brought on by the drainpipe, not fitting together correctly. This is a relatively simple thing for you to learn how to repair (watch some YouTube videos to discover how) or employ a plumbing professional, which should cost approximately $100.

4. Water Drip from Faucets - A slow drip from a sink or bathroom can end up costing you hundreds of dollars per year. If you have a sluggish drip, get it repaired right away. In most cases, the issue can be fixed with a $.50 rubber washer and about an hour of work by a plumber (or you). However, occasionally, the whole faucet will have to be replaced. If this valid, do not buy the $18 valve that is mainly plastic. You'll just be tearing it out next soon and changing it again and again.

5. No Hot Water - If the occupant loses their hot water, it's likely a problem with the warm water heater. You'll spend around $600 for a plumber to change it if they need a new hot water heating unit. It may just be the heating part inside the heating unit, in which case you can either replace it yourself for $20 and some working hours or employ a plumbing technician for a few hundred bucks to do it for you.

6. Bugs/Rodents - Dealing with insects can be one of the most irritating tasks for a property manager, because much of the time, it's the occupant's fault because they are unclean! Bugs and rodents like crumbs, so tenants with clean houses occasionally have an issue. That said, it's still your responsibility to make sure that any problem is taken care of. We tackle this question on two fronts: telling the tenant and working with an insect specialist to deal with the issue, which typically costs a couple of hundred dollars. Be sure to seal up any holes, no matter how little, that rodents or bugs could use to get into the property. Many property managers include in their lease that insect control is the occupant's responsibility after some weeks. This method, the property owner, can say that it was definitively not the property's issue but should be the occupant's. I discover this works in single-family houses, but in multifamily units, it can be impossible to find out where the bugs stemmed from because they take a trip through walls quickly.

7. Trash Disposals - These technological wonders might be fantastic for grinding up food in your home, but they are a continuous thorn in the side of property managers. They break all the time! Because tenants, I believe this is mostly put things into them that never belong in a waste disposal unit. (" I didn't know I wasn't supposed to put entire chicken bones down there!") For this factor, I try to remove waste disposal unit from my properties whenever possible. If your trash disposal breaks while an occupant is in the property and you require to repair it, there are usually two things that could be wrong. First, it might just be "stuck" and requires an Allen wrench to unstick it. Or the motor might be stressed out, in which case, you'll require a brand-new disposal, which might run a couple hundred dollars, including setup by a handyman.

8. Toilet Water Leaks - Toilets might be made from lasting porcelain, however the tank parts are typically low-cost pieces of plastic that break all the time. If a toilet is running (water can be heard going through it 24/7, or the tank refills with water by itself once in awhile), it's probably an issue with the flapper. Typically, these type of problems can be repaired with less than $20 in parts and an hour of labor by a plumber, handyman, or you.

9. Clogged Toilet - If your occupant blockages their toilet, this is not your responsibility. Issues that are triggered by the tenant are the tenant's obligation, so inform them that they require to call a plumber to handle the issue. Or call a plumbing yourself and bill the tenant for the cost. Nevertheless, if the drains appear to be clogged in the bath tub or bathroom sink also, this is a great indication that the issue might lie with your drain pipeline, such as a collapsed pipe or a tree root that has actually grown through it. (I once had a renter who flushed huge rocks down the toilet! This caused a major problem for me-- and led to a significant plumbing technician's costs!).

10. Heating System Repairs - Heat is vital, so a furnace repair work (specifically during the winter season) is one of the most essential repair work on this list. If a heater heads out, it could be something as easy as the pilot light going out or as complicated as a gas leak. When your tenant calls, get a furnace repair specialist out to the property immediately. Numerous heating system issues would have never happened had the heating system filter been changed often, so be sure your renter understands how and when to do this.

You'll likely encounter more issues than I've noted here while owning rental properties, but these ten concerns will likely represent 99% of the concerns you'll deal with. None of them, on their own, are that pricey to repair. If left untreated, each of these can end up costing you thousands or even 10s of thousands of dollars in damage. Treat each of these items with care and resolve them immediately. Your occupant, and your wallet, will thank you.

Property Owner Versus Tenant Responsibilities.

Not all repairs are the duty of the proprietor. Your job is to supply a safe, habitable property that depends on code. Unless your regional jurisdiction specifically requires it, you do not have to provide brand-new paint if a tenant's kid draws all over the wall. If the occupant tears it, you don't need to fix a piece of torn carpet. Because the occupant doesn't like the color, you don't require to offer new blinds. Unless your lease or local laws need you to repair these items, doing so depends on you.

Nevertheless, items such as smoke alarm, heat, appliances, pipes, these are your responsibilities to keep. I advise that you get a copy of your state's landlord-tenant laws and read them completely to understand what is, and is not, required in your location. Moreover, repairs that are required since the tenant broke something can be made the responsibility of the occupant. If an occupant breaks a window while moving some furniture, you are not accountable for the expense. Nevertheless, unless you desire your window covered with cardboard and duct-tape for the next six months, you might wish to employ the specialist to fix the issue and bill the occupant (I highly recommend that!) While the landlord absolutely has certain responsibilities with regard to the condition of the property, so does the occupant. It is the renter's obligation to report problems when they occur, and if they do not, the expense of fixing those problems could be placed on the renter (depending upon your state's laws). Your occupant likewise must keep the property safe and reasonably tidy and make sure they don't abuse the systems in the property, such as by overwhelming electrical outlets or flushing large items down a toilet.

Yearly Preventative Maintenance.

In addition to fixing problems when they happen, there is another category of repair work that as a property owner, you'll require to ensure gets done: preventative maintenance. In other words, these are jobs that require to be achieved on a routine basis, normally each year, whether or not anything is broken. They are preventative measures, not necessarily repair work.

Accomplishing these projects every year will keep your property's future repair work requires to a minimum and permit your property to run like a well-oiled machine. It will assist you conserve cash in time, because you'll find problems before they become a concern. I suggest giving the following list to your handyman once a year for each system you own. Bear in mind, this list is just a sample of a few of the continuous property upkeep you might need to do. Not all will apply to your.

property, and your property might have extra concerns. But this is a great place to start.

Interior.

When per year), Change heater filters (probably more than.

Vacuum dust from refrigerator coils.

Replace smoke alarm batteries.

Inspect to ensure carbon monoxide detector is set up and working.

Sweep the fireplace.

Ensure that lint from the dryer vent has a clear path to outdoors.

Flush water heating system.

Inspect expiration date on fire extinguisher.

Fix any damaged grout or caulk in restroom.

Tighten up any manages, knobs, racks, etc.

Remove showerheads and clean sediment.

Inspect weather removing on all doors and windows, and repair work as needed.

Exterior.

Clean rain gutters and get rid of all leaves and junk from inside.

Inspect siding and roof for noticeable signs of issues.

Check sump pump and make certain it is still operational.

Test garage door opener, including auto-reverse function.

Examine window screens and repair work as needed.

Look for signs of termites or other bugs.

Check trees for power line disturbance.

Repair any doors or windows as needed.

Cut up the landscaping.

Examine the crawl area; appearance for bugs and water leaks.

Touch up peeling or harmed paint.

Fertilize the lawn.

Shut off any openings to the crawlspace.

Inspect water valves (in both the fall and spring).

Wash exterior with garden hose pipe and mildew cleaner.

By executing this preventative upkeep checklist each year, you will have the ability to catch issues before they end up being pricey repairs while at the very same time keeping your property looking great. Plus, your tenants will appreciate your dedication to helping their home look and operate the finest. It's a true win-win.

Dealing With Difficult Tenants

Among the hardest parts of being a property manager is hand tough occupants. Nobody delights in conflict or drama. Unless you outsource your tenant communication to a property supervisor, you will have to anticipate dealing with such scenarios yourself.

Usually, the best way to lessen drama with most tenants is through appropriate tenant screening and allowing just the very best tenants to lease from you. Even with the greatest screening requirements and practices, bad occupants will make their way into your property. The next best method of reducing bad tenants is by successfully training them.

Training Your Tenants

Effectively training your tenants can make all the distinction between achieving success in real estate and being definitely unpleasant. Tenants need to be poked and prodded into accepting the will of the owner. How do you train a tenant? Regardless of the desire, definitely not with a big stick! Tenants are trained in several ways including; by developing rules, benefit etiquette, and using penalty when such rules are broken. The very first action is developing your rules by means of the lease contract. Ensure your tenant has a copy of their lease which includes all the rules and terms you wish to be complied. Make sure you implement them! Similar to when a bad mother and father decline to penalize their kid for misbehaving and end up with a bad kid on their hands, when you stop working to implement a set of rules for your tenant, you will eventually find yourself dealing with self-centred and uncooperative tenants.

Despite how well you screen and train, you will still have to deal with issues as they develop. The simplest method of penalizing tenants is through charges-- late costs, noncompliance charges, and so on. Now, a lot of proprietors battle with using charges, specifically when the tenant calls and say they can't pay rent due to the fact that "so-and-so" has this illness or their car broke down or they lost some money at work. It is not the property owner's task to be charitable. You will find that when your policy is to never budge on the rent or lease, unexpectedly all those reasons or excuses simply vanish.

CHAPTER EIGHT

Types of Real Estate Investment

In the real estate industry today, there are quite a variety of individuals that are associated with some kind of investment technique. There are now millions that have actually made this specific field of investment a complete profession and are doing extremely well with it. As there are numerous different opportunities in which one might be effective in this process, one need to understand the various kinds of real estate investment in order to understand which one is ideal for them.

Within this industry, the chances are typically endless if one is clever and mindful. Generally, each type does have a fundamental threat included which must be completely analyzed and understood before getting too deep into the process. The possibility to be effective really is unlimited when thoroughly evaluated and effectively followed.

In any process that is adopted, there are still a couple of standards and concepts that must be remembered. Going through this process might require a lot of capital in addition to a high level of discipline and perseverance. Short or long term chances need to constantly be kept in mind.

Commercial homes are becoming really common in the world of investment. Getting and renting out business property structures is usually highly financially rewarding and provides a regular stream of income on a continuous basis. This process frequently requires rather rigid insurance coverage and guidelines to be put in place in order to be safe and legal.

Rental homes are likewise a really common form of investing for many people. Today, this is typically in the format of homes, houses, and apartments that have actually been acquired on a rented basis. This is usually something carried out after it has been bought and lived in for some time after purchase.

House flipping is an extremely rewarding service for lots of people around the world. Purchasing depreciated and underestimated property and making it appealing and modern often generates an extraordinary earnings and offers an enjoyable work for those that do it. Hence, this field of investing is in fact becoming a lot more common today.

If carried out and dealt with thoroughly, owning land is really profitable and offers an attractive rate of return. When owning a plot of land of any sort, it has the ability to be sectioned off and offered in plots in relation to zoning laws and other typical features. Or, merely purchasing low value land and then offering it for increased revenue rates is likewise common and usually effective when offered to bigger corporations and services.

For those that are rather limited on capital, the buying of shares and stocks of property groups and investment jobs is common. Often, this offers similar appeal as a shared fund which is understood to generate a high rate of return in a lot of cases. Hence, in order to make sure this achieves success, ensure a total and directed success rate of the business being bought is well understood before deciding to make this kind of investment.

Knowing More About The Different Types of Real Estate Investment

If you are a new investor in the real estate market, then having a good understanding about the various kinds of real estate investment would go a long way in helping you make smart choices. Yes, when you understand this, you can successfully optimize your opportunities of making sensible income through such financial investments.

The various types of real estate investment include:

- **Residential**: In this kind of investment, we are describing the houses, apartment, condominiums, townhouses and other kinds of houses where the residents pay to live alone or with their families. The length of time they remain is generally contained or described in the rent or lease agreement between you and them.

- **Retail:** This describes shops, shopping malls and strip malls. In this kind of investment, the structures are developed or purchased and rented for the sole function of working as retail outlets for different kinds of services to business owners at agreed rates.

- **Commercial:** This is where the office complexes or buildings actually come in. When it concerns real estate investment, you can make a lot of money by building or purchasing developed property with private workplaces which are consequently rented or leased to small business owners or corporations.

- **Industrial:** This is the kind of property that is comprised of unique function systems like storage systems, car wash and lots more. They are mostly known for producing high income from rendering specific services to clients who want to use the properties. In the car wash system, you can have an ice vending device or a coin-operated vacuum cleaner which goes even more to optimize the earning capacities of such investment.

- **Mixed Use:** Among the numerous kinds of real estate investment, this specific one is really different. It is usually ideal for those who own substantial assets. It is about integrating numerous classifications of real estate financial investments and forming them into one, with the exclusion of residential type. You can develop or purchase a property that caters for retail, commercial and service providers. If for instance, the property is a 3-storey structure, you can lease out the ground floor to a bank, the 2nd floor to an insurance provider and the remaining floors to other business types. You can construct stores around the property and lease them out to hair beauty parlors, confectioners, health club and others. There need to be an integrated diversity so that every company has its own significant entryway in order to decrease and at the same time, manage the significant risks of doing business in a mixed used property.

Now that you are mindful of all these, you are fit o go as far as real estate investment is concerned, even as a new investor.

Kinds of Real Estate Investment Properties

Real estate investing techniques have actually gone through significant modifications in recent years. Prior to the banking crisis and financial recession, lots of investors were generating enormous earnings through engaging and rehabbing distressed residential or commercial properties in flipping of house. Today, investors are using distressed residential or commercial properties to create rental income or to use imaginative funding choices.

The primary step to accomplishing real estate investment success is by being informed about the marketplace. Investors must be knowledgeable about the numerous kinds of investment homes such as domestic, industrial, and vacant land, along with buying real estate notes and land contracts.

Residential real estate can also be used as rental properties or outrightly offered for sale. Lots of investors are providing imaginative financing methods to draw in purchasers who can not get approved for bank funding. Popular funding options consist of lease purchase options agreements and seller carry back forms of mortgages.

Industrial real estate consists of a large mix of homes such as condo and apartment building, storage facilities, retail stores, and office buildings. When acquiring business property in order to cover the expenses and management tasks needed to preserve investment homes, investors often partner with other investors or investment groups.

Commercial property has the prospective to create considerable revenues as long as investors analyze market conditions. Investors might be entitled to tax rewards when business financial investments bring job opportunity to the location or when residential or commercial properties are updated utilizing energy-efficient innovation such as photovoltaic panels or other types of green energy.

Since this type of real estate is often priced below market value, investors mostly look for bank owned foreclosure residential or commercial properties. Bank owned real estate includes all kinds of homes and can vary from mobile houses to fancy commercial parks and high-rise houses to golf courses.

Finding commercial and residential foreclosures is reasonably easy. Using the services of a real estate agent can accelerate the process. Agents can have access to the Multiple Listings (MLS) database to rapidly find all kinds of residential or commercial properties for sale.

When banks reclaim homes they are very first positioned for sale through public or federal government auctions. If it goes unsold at auction, the property is provided back to the bank. Banks then offer foreclosure residential or commercial properties through their loss mitigation department or regional real estate agents.

Costs of bank owned homes are usually greater than residential or commercial properties offered through auction. Banks eliminate liens and judgments in order to offer the real estate with a good title. Purchasers have the ability to take fast ownership and can move on with preparing the property for sale or lease.

Investors who buy industrial real estate need to get informed about federal, state, and other related property laws. Industrial structures need to abide by the Disability laws as well as other applicable enactments and be zoned for business usage.

The real estate market continues to head in a down spiral and there are still plenty of strong investment opportunities. As much as possible, investors need to remain abreast of market conditions and be capable of altering techniques. Otherwise, they will rapidly end up being just another real estate statistics.

When investing in rental homes, knowledge and understanding can be helpful in reducing the danger attached with it. The much better you know and understand the marketplace, your investment, and how to handle that investment, the lower the risks that something will fail. If you do the proper calculations before you purchase an investment property and understand that you need to account for the property sitting empty at a particular part of the year, then when it takes place, it will not have much negative impact on your base line. It's simply part of the business. Your knowledge and understanding can help protect your investment against the important things that will fail.

Difficulties of Rental Property Investment

Real estate investment is not always fun and it is desirable for any interested investor to understand both the positives and negatives before leaping in. Certainly, this is not an attempt to discourage you, but it's crucial that you understand the tune before beginning the dance. The following list describes a few of the main problems, risks and inconveniences of being a rental property investor as well as some ideas on how to deal with them.

1. Building or Creating Wealth Takes Time

Of course, great wealth has been created by those who have rental properties. However, such wealth has never been created or built overnight. On the contrary, creating wealth via real estate is basically about taking consistent step or action over a considerable length of time. The significant keywords here are "consistent step or action" and "considerable length of time." Are you well prepared to start or get in this game for the long time? Are you prepared for the ups and the downs likely to come with your rental properties? If you are, then you may proceed.

2. It Can Become All Consuming

The Rental property investment has a likelihood or tendency of taking over your life, just as any venture based on passion can. For example, a couple sitting down for their dinner each night may find it a bit difficult to not talk about their rentals. When a rental property investor lies in bed at night, he may have to force himself to not think about all the moving parts. Even when such investor is watching TV, he may find himself thinking, "Hmmm, I just wonder what the rent of that beautiful apartment would cost…"

3. Dealing with Difficult People.

As a rental property investor or owner, you are definitely not an island. You are always involved with other people!

From deadbeat tenants to contractors to bankers and other difficult individuals, at some point, you will have to relate with difficult people in some situations. You may be left with no choice but to fire a particular contractor who fails to show up on time. You may just need to let your property manager go when such a person can't help fill a vacancy fast enough. You might have to deal with the same sob story about why the rent was late several times. At some point, you will probably end up evicting a tenant.

However, you need to understand that you can possibly limit your exposure to such difficult people through effective management. By effectively carrying out your due diligence to find a great property manager or contractor, you will reduce the likelihood of you having reasons to fire that person later. By taking time to screen your tenants very well, you will have the opportunity of weeding out the ones who are likely to cause you much damage. By outsourcing some tasks you don't feel like doing (such as showing vacant units and answering phone calls), you will be able to decrease your interaction with the difficult situations and people.

4. It Involves Bookkeeping and much of Paperwork

In the rental property business, it is common to involve a lot of paperwork in keeping track of transactions! From leases to insurance to forms to taxes, a large part of an investor's time is mostly spent on just putting the paperwork side of the business in order. An investor probably receives several pieces of mail each week that somehow involve rental properties, and each one of such mail needs to be opened, read, and filed.

Furthermore, when actively investing in rental properties, it is very necessary to maintain accurate bookkeeping and accounting records, which can be quite challenging. The QuickBooks software is not easy to learn, and if you choose to make use of spreadsheets, be ready to juggle many of them. Receipts have to be properly logged and filed, the contractors need to be paid and those charges have to be recorded as your taxes begin to take on a new level as your rental portfolio grows.

5. Your Investment Can Be Lost

Rental properties are forms of investment, and as common with all investments, there is a risk of you losing. Not all rental property owners end up being successful. In fact, it appears that most "mother and father" landlords eventually lose money due to the fact that they don't run a standard rental property business.

There are effective ways of reducing your risks and improving your chances for outstanding success. By taking out time to read this book and increasing your knowledge, you have already adopted one of such ways.

CHAPTER NINE

Inflation and How It Affects Your Investment

Every year, various economies across the globe tend to increase the money supply. As more money get to chase after a slowly increasing level of properties supply, the prices of properties go up—even in the absence of an overall positive change in the underlying forces of demand and supply (referred to as market appreciation).

Monetary policies are specifically designed by Government authorities to create a modest percentage of annual gain in the Consumer Price Index (CPI). Though, sometimes, the Government authorities lose control of inflationary price increases. During those high level inflationary times, the real estate prices will often experience increased percentage of inflationary gains.

Interest Rates and Inflation

Journalists and reporters have repeatedly spread the myth that the so-called "current historically low mortgage interest rates" are responsible for the recent price run-ups in housing.

In reality, the modern day's 30-year mortgage interest rates of 5 to 7 percent only seem low relative to those mortgage rates of 8 to 16 percent that was experienced throughout much of the 1970s and 1980s. So, today's inflation rates actually stand toward the high-average end of history-not the historically low. The crucial question one may ask is; what then happens to prices of real estate if the interest rates do go up?

Higher Interest Rates Are Mostly Caused by Higher Inflation

Long-term interest rates increased dramatically during the 1970s and 1980s simply because the Consumer Price Index (inflation) increased from the mild annual levels of about 2.5 to 4.0 percent of the early to mid-1960s all the way up to about 13 percent in the year 1982. And for the record, you probably can take note that during those years of increasing inflation and skyrocketing interest rates, most property values increased drastically.

Though, a higher inflation can drive up interest rates, inflation also drives up rent levels as well as the cost of construction.

More beneficial for real estate investors is the fact that when inflation goes up, the smart money raises financial assets (bonds and stocks) in favour of hard assets (including real estate). As a result, the prices of property are raised even higher as bond and stock prices stagnate or drop.

History proves that over long periods, higher interest rates do not hurt property values. On the contrary, higher interest rates propel prices of property to new heights.

Lower Interest Rates? Higher Interest Rates? You Gain Either Way

Assuming you purchase today and secure a long-term mortgage interest rate of about 6.5 percent, if interest rates go down, you can refinance and take advantage of lower payments.

Yet, if inflation again goes wild and interest rates head up to 8, 10, 12 percent or higher, you'll gain as inflation drives the price of your property up and slices the real amount of your mortgage balance. You borrow dollars when their purchasing power is strong. You pay them back when their buying power has fallen. You gain. Your lender loses. When rates go down, you can re-finance. When rates go up due to inflation, you can collect higher rents and pay your loan off in cheap dollars. Regardless of which direction interest rates move, real estate investors (mortgage borrowers) reap the gains for themselves.

CHAPTER TEN

Tax Tips and Tricks

It's clear, tax obligations can get complex. There are relatively countless guidelines from the tax authorities on what you can and cannot do as an investor as it relates to your tax obligations.

Tax obligations are intricate, though online articles have lots of complicated language, and individuals like you are losing out on placing even more money back right into your pockets. That's why this chapter is dedicated to looking at some essential tax ideas for genuine real estate investors in an easy-to-read, jargon-free context.

Have you ever seen somebody folding up an invoice and pushing it in their wallet after consuming a meal at a restaurant? It's possible that they were conserving that invoice to "cross out" the meal. There's an opportunity you might be able to recuperate the you pay if you're doing anything for the benefit of your business.

For instance, If you acquired $1,000 worth of drywall for a particular place you have, and you were asked to pay a 6% sales tax ($ 60), you would certainly be able to subtract that from the tax you will owe at the end of the year.

Tax reductions such as this aren't just booked for building and construction projects-- practically anything business related can be written off.

Below are some of the most frequently neglected expenditures you can cross out as an entrepreneur:

Mileage - Driving to and from various properties? If it's business-related, the tax authorities allow you write off some percentage of your expenses for every mile you cover on your car. Make sure to track your miles! Same goes with any other kind of traveling costs you have as a result of handling your real estate business (accommodations, airfare, dishes, etc).

Part of your home- You don't have a 'workplace'? not a problem. The IRS allows you write off a part of your home as a workplace. As an investor, you'll absolutely be doing a few of your business from home. This is a piece of cake deduction.

Obviously, there are actually two standard requirements for your home to qualify:

Exclusive and regular usage - "You need to always use part of your home solely for doing business. If you use an added space to run your business, you can take a home-office deduction for that additional space," the IRS says. The room cannot be made use of for personal purposes.

Principal place of your business- According to the IRS, "you have to show that you use your home as your primary place of business. If you carry out business at a place beyond your home, but likewise use your home significantly and consistently to do business, you might get an office deduction." Make sure to speak with your CPA for more analysis of the term "principal."

Interests - As you deal in properties, you're most likely to obtain loans, and those sort of loans will have some level of interest rates connected to them. The interesting part is that every one of the home mortgage interest, points, and home loan insurance coverage costs can really be written off as tax obligation deductions. It's crucial to keep in mind, that current legislations have actually established the limit of reductions of as much as $750K in home mortgage financial debt.

Expert Services - If you paid a property supervisor, attorney, accounting professional or any other kind of professional business, possibilities are you can write it off as long as the service was straight pertaining to your rental investment property.

Depreciation- As your property experiences wear and tear, the IRS lets you assert that your property will certainly drop over 27.5 years. This implies that annually, the quantity of the worth of your "renovations" (such as capital investment, significant property improvements like changing a roofing or completing your basement) separated by 27.5 can be subtracted from ordinary taxable income for 27.5 years. Translation: You possess the potential to minimize the quantity of income tax you pay as a result of depreciation.

CONCLUSION

If you have the mind for real estate or wish to employ somebody who does. Then you must forego a large part of your portfolio to purchase realty. It is regarded as one of the investments with highest returns worldwide, the only caveat, like anything else, is that you need to do it right to be effective.

The real estate market is not static; it changes. It's affected by the general economy; it's affected by the political climate; it's affected by a range of local issues. You need to know what to do in any market, and then you will always be in the right place at the right time. This book explains certain techniques that will work in almost every market and others that will work under certain conditions. Armed with that knowledge, you'll be able to develop a consistently profitable investment strategy.

As long as you buy real estate with a positive cash flow—that is, as long as the property generates more revenue than it costs you to own it—you'll be able to ride out any economic downturn because you'll never buy any- thing you're not willing to hold for five to seven years.

Above all, take time to read this book thoroughly. The relevant details have been provided and you would need to create a shortlist of the essential things you need to put in place before you proceed to make an offer. That includes taking time to do background checks on the market that you are targeting and preparing the house for such market, knowing fully well that the market is vibrant enough. With that, you get a satisfying feeling which spurs you on toward the next project and a lot more because that's what flipping houses is all about. The next challenge will always offer even more scope than the last one did. People in the real estate business don't easily give up. They just get better and much better at doing what they are good at.

CPSIA information can be obtained
at www.ICGtesting.com
Printed in the USA
BVHW040255121120
592963BV00021B/120

9 781801 200264